amazing FAITH

TESTIMONIES OF
FAITH & PERSEVERANCE

TRICIA CRAIB

amazing FAITH

TESTIMONIES OF FAITH & PERSEVERANCE

MEMOIRS
Cirencester

Published by Memoirs

MEMOIRS
PUBLISHING

25 Market Place, Cirencester, Gloucestershire, GL7 2NX
info@memoirsbooks.co.uk www.memoirspublishing.com

Amazing Faith

Testimonies of Faith and Perseverence

ISBN: 978-1-909544-31-4

For the staff at the International Christian College, Glasgow

TABLE OF CONTENTS

❧

Foreword

❧

ACKNOWLEDGEMENTS

Firstly I would like to thank all those in this book who shared their testimonies with me. It was a real privilege to write their stories. Secondly I could not have produced this book without a lot of help and encouragement from friends and family especially husband Kenny and daughter Julie. I am deeply grateful to my sister Eileen and friends Anne and Meryl for their hard work proof-reading the manuscript. Also daughters Louisa, Susan, son-in-law Sam and friend Byron for working on the photographs. My son Kenneth also helped with his computer skills for which I am thankful. Thanks also to Charles and Jo at Diadem for their help. Finally I am indebted to Laura who produced the lovely illustrations at short notice.

FOREWORD

You could say this is a great book about some people who have experienced God at work in wonderful ways in their lives. Or you could say this is a book about some great people who have seen God at work in wonderful ways in their lives. Or you could say this is a book about some people who have experienced a great God at work in wonderful ways in their lives. And all these things are true about this book.

The stories in this book will take you around the world, to Nepal, Thailand and Mongolia in Asia, and to Uganda in Africa. As you read them you'll find yourself transported in your head to these very different places, where life is often much more difficult than it is for people in the West. You'll read about different customs. Some of them, like marriage introductions, may seem strange to you. Some of them, like needing to watch out that wild animals like jackals and tigers don't attack, may seem a bit scary. Some of them, like being forced to leave your home village because you're a Christian, may seem sad. But you'll also read about how God watches over people, even in the toughest situations.

I got to know three of the people you will meet in these stories— Chitra, Kenneth and Honey—when they were students at International Christian College, where I teach. But one of the things

I really like about this book is that it gave me a chance to find out how God had been at work in their lives, long before they even knew Him or believed in Jesus. I learned about God's care for them and their families and how, even when there seemed to be little hope, God was watching over them. And it made me very moved as I saw that God was in control of their lives and kept leading them as they followed Him faithfully. So, yes, this is a great book, and I'm really glad that Tricia has written these stories so well for us to enjoy.

As I read the stories, and as you read them, you'll be amazed, as I was, at how courageous these people are. You'll read about how they stayed true to Jesus even if it meant they had to leave their home, or if it meant they were the odd one out at school, or if it meant they had to forgive someone who'd done them harm. You'll be amazed also at how they have been brave enough to go to new places and sometimes to learn new languages because they believed God had called them to go there. So, yes, you'll think, as I do, that these are great people.

And we might also think, "I could never do the kind of things that Chitra or Kenneth or Brasit or Honey have done." But there was a time when they thought they could never do them either. All the people in this book would say they were only able to do what they did because God is a great God, and He gave them the faith and the courage to follow Him. And they would also say that it's because of Jesus' love for them and for the whole world that they want to serve Him, and to tell His Good News to as many people as they can. So, above all this is a book about a *great God*.

As you read these stories I hope there's something else that you'll notice. The heroes of these stories are Chitra, Kenneth, Brasit and

Honey. But other people appear here as well, other Christians, who have a big impact on the lives of these four people. They have an impact by the way that they show God's love to them, and by the way they pray for them, and by the way they are generous with their money in helping to provide for their needs and to support their work.

So, as you read these great stories about these great people, my prayer is that you'll have a heart that's open to what God might want to say to you through them. It might be that He'll call you to do something great for Him, perhaps even to go and serve Him in another country. But as we read we will certainly all be reminded of what God wants for all people, which is to love Him, to be open to His voice as we pray, to love other people, and to be generous with the things He has given to us. As we read these stories we'll want to give thanks to God for what He has done, and what He will do, in the lives of Chitra, Kenneth, Brasit and Honey, and in our lives too. And just like Tricia thought as she wrote about God's work in these people's lives, we'll want to say, "To God be the glory!"

Now, enough from me, let's get reading.
David Miller
International Christian College, July 2012.

The old hut in the forest

Watch Out for the Monkeys!

CHAPTER ONE

"I DON'T LIKE IT HERE," whispered Devi to her brother Chitra as they walked up to the old hut.

"I don't like it either," replied Chitra.

"It feels creepy. Why are there no other families living here?" Devi asked Chitra in a low voice. Chitra looked about the place.

"I don't know," answered Chitra. "All I know is that our father's family used to live here. When his father died the family went to another village. Perhaps that is why no-one lives here now."

Deu Kumari, their mother, arrived at the hut. She wiped the sweat from her brow, and opened the door.

"Why do we have to live here?" Devi asked her mother as they went into the empty hut.

"We have no choice, Devi," said her mother sadly. She

put her bag down on the floor. In it were a few things they had brought with them. These were their only possessions.

"Chitra, take Devi with you and look about the place," ordered their mother. "See what you can find to eat. Perhaps there are some nettles growing in the woods over there. I think there is a stream nearby. Take a look around and let me know what you find."

"I'm tired from walking all this way," cried Devi, sitting down on the floor.

"So am I," sighed Chitra, sitting beside his sister.

"All right, rest a while. I will go and look around. Stay here till I come back," she cautioned.

"It's cold in here," said Devi after her mother had left.

She shivered and moved nearer her big brother. She knew her mother was sad and didn't want to be here either.

Chitra and Devi sat on the dirt floor waiting for their mother to come back. There was nothing in the old hut, no chairs, no table and no bed. The hut had a strange smell about it like old smoky wood. A hole in the roof for the smoke to go out let the only light into the dark room.

"What if Mummy doesn't come back?" said Devi after some time.

"Don't be silly, Devi. She wouldn't leave us here all alone," replied Chitra trying to sound reassuring.

Then they heard the sound of footsteps and their mother came in the door.

"Don't just sit there, you two!" she shouted at them. "Go and get some wood for a fire or there will be no food for you tonight."

Chitra and Devi jumped up and ran off into the woods nearby.

"Here, make a pile of wood by this tree," ordered Chitra, "and don't get wet wood. It won't burn."

Devi looked about the forest floor and picked up all the small, dry bits of wood.

"Why is everyone so angry and sad?" she thought to herself as she ran to the pile Chitra had made by the tree. She put down her armful of sticks. Then she went to look for some more. She was afraid to ask any more questions as she realised her brother was in a bad mood now too. Tears filled her eyes as she tried to find more sticks.

"Maybe Chitra will be pleased with me if I make a big pile of wood," she thought to herself. She sniffed back the tears and ran about searching for dry sticks. Just as she was putting down her bundle of wood Chitra threw a large branch onto the pile. The branch hit Devi on the head. She fell down crying. Chitra came running over to his sister.

"I'm sorry, I didn't mean to hit you. I didn't see you there at the tree. Are you all right?" he asked, wiping the blood from her head with his dirty sleeve. "Don't cry Devi, I didn't mean to hurt you."

"Why is everyone so sad and angry?" sobbed Devi, wiping her face with her hand. "Why did Daddy hit Mummy and send us away to this horrible place? I wish we were staying at Granny's hut. Why can't we stay with Granny, Chitra?"

Chitra rubbed the ground with his bare foot. He was only a little boy. He didn't understand what was going on. How could a six-year-old boy explain why they had to live in such an awful place?

"I don't know," he said at last. "All I know is we are to stay here and try to grow some food for us to eat. Father does not want us in his home. He has a new wife and other children now. We will just have to help Mother as best we can."

"It feels like there are dead spirits here!" said Devi in alarm.

"No there's not," said Chitra angrily, "but it is a strange place and I don't like it much. I think Mother is scared here too. Come on, I think we have enough wood for a fire. We can take this bundle back to Mother then go and look for berries and nettles in the woods."

Chitra and Devi left the pile of wood by the door of their hut and went back into the forest to look for some nettles.

"Look!" shouted Chitra. "There are nettles over by that clearing."

"How are we going to pick them?" asked Devi as she looked at the patch of nettles. "We don't have the tongs we used at our old hut. Nettles sting your hands, don't they?"

"Yes, you must pick them very carefully, catching them at the root," Chitra said. "Try not to touch the leaves."

Devi tried to pick the nettles but they hurt her hands.

"Ouch!" she cried and sat down on the ground. "I can't do it."

"I know what to do," said Chitra. "I'll pick them and you can carry them in your daura.[1] See, hold the ends of your daura and I will put the nettles into it."

Soon Chitra had gathered lots of nettles. Devi carried them carefully making sure she didn't drop any. On the way back to the old hut Chitra found some berries which he carried in his shirt.

"I think I saw the stream over by the clearing," said Devi. "I'll get some water after we take the nettles to Mother. She will need the water to cook the nettles."

"Yes," said Chitra. "Mother is hot and tired. She can rest while I run back for some more firewood. Then I will make

1. Daura-Suruwal, or Daura Suruwal, is a national costume of Nepal.

the fire while you get the water."

"I'll try to be brave and not cry, Chitra. I will try very hard," sighed Devi.

The children brought the berries and nettles to their mother who was sitting by the door of the old hut cleaning some vegetables. She got up and went into the hut followed by the children.

"Thank you children," she said as they dropped the berries and the nettles onto the floor.

"We have gathered some firewood too," said Devi happily.

"You rest here, Mother, while I go back for some more wood and Devi goes for some water," said Chitra.

"I'll prepare the nettles," replied their mother. She went to her bundle of things and took out a big metal bowl and a jug which she handed to Devi. Then she sat down beside the pile of nettles and began to pick off the top blossoms. Carefully she put them into the bowl.

The children went off to get more wood and some water.

"At least we were able to bring this big jug with us," said Devi running out of the hut with the jug in her hand. "How could we get water if we had nothing to carry it in?"

"Yes, that's true," laughed Chitra. "Just as well Daddy let us take some things with us before he threw us out. We have a blanket to lie on and a pot to cook things in. We have all we need."

"Don't forget the kodalo and the hasiya. Mother could not dig the ground if we didn't have a kodalo," added Devi.

"And I wouldn't be able to cut the grass or chop the wood without a hasiya," laughed Chitra.

A kodalo and a hasiya used for cutting and digging

Chitra and Devi felt better as they hurried back to the forest while their mother prepared the nettles.

"I found the stream!" shouted Devi, running into the hut some time later. "Here is some water, Mother."

Deu Kumari stopped what she was doing and came over to Devi.

"Oh thank you, Devi. I'm very thirsty. It's been a long day walking here," said Deu Kumari, taking the jug from Devi. She drank some of the water then handed the jug back to Devi.

"Chitra will make the fire when he gets back," said Devi. "I'll go and get some more water so that you can cook the nettles."

"Thank you," said her mother taking a big pot out of her bag. "You can put the rest of the water in this pot. I have some vegetables to cook with the nettles. We'll have soup for dinner."

Devi poured the water from the jug into the pot. Deu Kumari picked up the bowl with the nettles and put the vegetables into the bowl. She handed it to Devi.

"Take this with you and thoroughly clean the nettles and vegetables in the stream. We don't want any dirt or insects in our soup. When everything is washed I will cut them up and put them in the pot," she said.

"Chitra can help you cut up the vegetables," suggested Devi.

6

"Yes he could, but he will have to be very careful," said Deu Kumari. "We don't want a cut finger. There's no one to help us out here, remember, so don't do anything silly."

Just then Chitra came into the hut carrying a bundle of wood. He started to make the fire while Devi ran to the stream.

Deu Kumari put the pot over the fire to boil the water. When Devi returned with the washed vegetables and nettles and more water, her mother added them to the pot. Then she thickened the soup with some maize flour. As soon as the soup had cooled they sat down on the hard ground to drink it. The smell of the burning wood reminded Chitra of meals shared with a large community of friends and family back in their village. He felt very lonely in this place with only his mother and sister.

"Be careful not to spill any of the soup down your shirt, Chitra," warned his mother as she poured some of the soup into his waiting cupped hands. Devi's hands shook as she waited for her mother to put some of the soup into her tiny dirty hands. Devi slurped the soup quickly into her mouth, then held out her hands for more. After the soup was finished they both still felt hungry, even after eating the berries they had found in the forest.

That night they huddled together under the blanket in the old hut at the edge of the forest and tried to sleep.

CHAPTER TWO

DEU KUMARI made a home for her family. She found a field about a mile away from the old hut. There she tilled the ground and grew some maize which she was able to sell at the market. With the money she was able to buy five goats that she kept tethered near the hut. The little family had survived living in what was actually the hut where their grandfather had died!

One day Chitra's mother was going to the market with some vegetables. She took Devi with her. As she was leaving she called, "Chitra, go to the maize field and keep watch. Don't let the monkeys come near the maize. And take the goats with you. Perhaps they will find some nice sweet grass in the forest. I am off to the market with Devi. Keep watching for those monkeys! The maize is nearly ready to pick and they know there is food there." Deu Kumari picked up her bag and began to walk away. She turned round and said, "We will pick the maize next week and sell it at the market. Then we can buy some maize flour to last us till the next lot of vegetables grow. Pay attention to what you are doing, Chitra. We will be back before nightfall."

"I'll keep watch Mother. Don't worry, I will keep the monkeys away. Bye," said Chitra as he watched them go into the woods.

Chitra walked along the path to their field prodding the goats in front of him. When he arrived at the field he walked round it swinging his stick in the air to warn the monkeys he was in charge. "Don't come near our field or I will hit you with this stick!" he shouted up at the monkeys in the trees. The monkeys chattered loudly as if laughing at Chitra. The goats wandered off into the nearby forest.

It was very hot and Chitra grew tired. He had not slept well since coming to this place. He sat down by the edge of the field and looked up into the trees. The monkeys had disappeared deeper into the shade of the forest. Suddenly it began to rain and Chitra jumped up to see where the goats were. He looked around in the forest near the field but the goats were not there! He called to the goats and listened for their cry. He called again but the goats did not answer.

"Oh, where have those stupid goats got to?" Chitra asked himself. "I'm soaking wet and now I will have to go and look for them. Mother will be very angry if I have lost them."

Chitra set off through the woods to look for the goats. At last he heard a cry and followed the sound to a cave in the rocks above the stream where the goats were sheltering from the rain. Chitra crawled into the cave. It was warm and dry there. He sat down by one of the goats and rested against her soft side. Two of the kids jumped on his back. Chitra pushed them off and lay down on the floor of the cave. The kids jumped onto his tummy. Soon he was fast asleep curled up beside the goats.

It was getting dark when Chitra woke up. He ran out of the cave chasing the goats in front of him. He ran back to the field as fast as he could. The goats bleated angrily as they were hurried along the path. Chitra stopped abruptly as he reached the maize field. He could not believe his eyes!

There, in the dim light of evening, he could make out the monkeys eating the maize. He rushed into the field shouting and waving his arms about. The monkeys fled to the nearby trees screeching loudly.

Tears were running down his face as Chitra looked about him. Only a few stalks of maize were left in the field. Chitra was about to run away, fearing the wrath of his mother, when he heard a scream. His mother had returned!

The monkeys ruined the maize

"What have you done, you wicked boy!" she yelled as she ran into the field.

Devi ran and hid behind some trees. Chitra cowered as his mother approached. He knew he deserved the beating he was about to get. There was no use trying to explain.

Sometime later Chitra crept out of the field. It was night, but the moon shone down on the destroyed maize field. Chitra walked slowly back to the hut. Although it was dark he was able to find his way along the familiar path by the light of the moon. Half an hour later he arrived home. He went quietly into the hut and lay down beside Devi.

"Are you all right?" she whispered to Chitra as she put her arm round his shoulder.

"Yes," whispered Chitra. Devi tried to comfort her big brother but she could feel him sobbing as he lay beside her.

The next morning Deu Kumari was still angry and sad. They walked to the field in silence.

"What are we going to do now?" she cried, looking at the mess. Most of the maize had gone and the stalks were broken and trampled on by the monkeys. To make matters worse the monkeys were up in the trees nearby, chattering happily, laughing at poor Chitra.

"I'm so sorry Mother," said Chitra, looking at the destruction in front of him. "It began to rain and I went to look for the goats. The monkeys must have been watching and as soon as I left they must have come down."

"More likely you fell asleep or ran off to play," replied Deu Kumari angrily. "What are we going to do now?" she repeated sadly. "There is no maize to sell at the market and the vegetables are not ready yet. We will all starve to death because of you!"

Poor Chitra felt awful. It was entirely his fault. If he hadn't fallen asleep he would have got back before the monkeys had eaten all the maize. Now they had no food, no money and his mother was very angry with him. Chitra didn't know what to do. He picked up the hasiya and went to cut some grass for the goats.

"If I get some nice sweet grass for the goats they will produce good fresh milk for us," thought Chitra. "I'll look for some nuts and berries as well. There are still some nettles growing for the soup. I will make sure we don't starve till the vegetables have grown," Chitra promised himself.

Somehow the little family survived till the vegetables were ready, but they were often hungry. When they sold the vegetables, Deu Kumari was able to buy more maize to plant.

CHAPTER THREE

"**COME ON**, we'll be late for school Devi!" shouted Chitra as he picked up his piece of wood. He went to the fire and took out some of the charcoal left from the burning wood. He rubbed his piece of wood with the charcoal, then put the charcoal in his pocket. He ran out of the door and into the forest.

"Wait for me!" cried Devi, running to catch up with her big brother.

"I'm so pleased to be going back to school," said Chitra. "It is good that you can come too now. You will like it. You will learn to read and write and I will cut a special piece of wood for you."

"Will you, Chitra? I want a piece of wood just like yours to write on," said Devi.

She skipped along the path for a little while, and then asked, "When will we be at the school?"

"It will take us about two hours Devi, so you can't stop on the way. It is further than the market you have been to with Mother," warned Chitra.

"Two hours! I won't be able to walk that far," said Devi,

suddenly realising that going to school may not be the fun she thought it would be.

"You'll get used to it after a time. There are lots of other children to play with at the school. We also get some rice to eat before we go back home. Come on, you need to keep up with me or you will be late on your first day," said Chitra, stooping down to pick up a stone.

"What do you want that stone for?" asked Devi.

"That is what you use to write on the wood," answered Chitra. "See, you scratch a mark on the charcoal and it leaves the wood showing through. That is how you write," explained Chitra. He made some marks on the wood with the stone and showed it to Devi.

"See, that is my name, and here is yours," he said, scratching the wood with the stone. "When you want to write something else you rub the wood with the charcoal and make more letters."

"I want to do that too!" said Devi excitedly. "I can't wait to get to school."

"Come on then, we need to run this bit," said Chitra, putting the stone and the charcoal in his pocket. "It's downhill, so it is easy. Come on."

The children went to school every day and Devi soon learned to read and write. It was difficult to do any schoolwork at home as there was no light in the old hut, but Chitra practiced his writing at the weekends and helped Devi as well. When Deu Kumari made some money selling her vegetables Chitra was able to buy a book for school. But life was still hard for the little family.

One day Deu Kumari called Chitra into the hut. She handed him the big pot.

"Take this pot to the blacksmith on your way to school," she said. "It has a hole in it. He will be able to fix it and you can get it on your way home. We need the pot to cook the soup," she added. Chitra took the pot then looked at his mother.

"Isn't the blacksmith from the untouchable caste?" he asked his mother.

"Yes, but they have to serve us, their masters. We need the pot repaired," she answered. "Now hurry along or you will be late for school. Tell him I will bring some grain when I'm next in the village."

Chitra had never been to the blacksmith's. He had never seen him work. He had always avoided going near his shop at the edge of the village.

When they arrived at the place where the blacksmith worked Chitra noticed the thick grey smoke rising from a big fire. The blacksmith was hammering a bit of metal. Chitra stood and watched his huge arms lift the big hammer. He shut his eyes every time the hammer hit the metal. Devi ran and hid behind her brother. She didn't like the noise or the smell or the hot fire. Chitra just looked at the blacksmith.

"Can I help you?" the blacksmith said after he had finished hammering.

"My mother needs this pot fixed. It has a hole in it," answered Chitra handing him the pot.

The blacksmith looked at the pot, turning it over.

"That's not a problem. I'll have it ready for you when you come back from school," said the blacksmith.

"My mother said she will bring you some grain when she next comes into the village," said Chitra as he walked away.

"It's just as well we are of a high caste," said Devi as they went on to school. "I wouldn't like to serve and work hard for other people."

After this first visit to the blacksmith's shop, Chitra often stopped on his way home from school to watch him working. One day the blacksmith said, "Come over here, I have something for you."

Chitra followed him to the back of the shop. The blacksmith handed Chitra a small metal bowl.

"This is for you," he said.

Chitra couldn't believe his eyes. He took the bowl in his hands, thanked the blacksmith and ran off home.

"Mother, Devi, look what the blacksmith gave me!" he said excitedly, showing them the bowl. "Now I won't need to drink my soup out of my hands. I have my own bowl. I won't spill any soup down my shirt, and my clothes won't get dirty."

Chitra was so pleased with his new bowl. It was one of the happiest days of his young life. He shared his precious bowl with Devi, allowing her to use it after he had drunk all his soup.

Eventually Deu Kumari and the children were able to move to Jungu, the village where their grandparents lived. There were other children to play with now and the field there produced more crops for them to sell. Deu Kumari worked hard in her field to provide for her two children. Chitra's jobs were still to look after the goats, gather and chop wood for the fire and help his mother in the maize field.

One day the children were playing in the trees nearby. They were trying to see who could climb up to the highest branch. Chitra was very good at climbing because he was small and light and was able to get up to the high branches. He shouted to the others below, "You are too scared to follow me, ha, ha! Come on. Try and catch me!" He laughed as he swung from branch to branch.

"You're just like a monkey," laughed Deu Kumari as she walked past the tree. "I hope you are looking after the goats."

Chitra suddenly remembered the goats. He climbed down from the tree and asked the other children if they had seen his goats.

"They were with the other goats over there among the trees," said one of the boys.

"I hope they aren't eating the crops in Bahadur's field. I will get into trouble if they have gone in there," said Chitra rushing off to look for the goats. The goats were not in Bahadur's garden. Chitra hunted for the goats till night-time but there was no sign of them anywhere.

"They must have wandered off into the forest," Chitra told his mother when he came home without the goats.

"Well, you had better find them tomorrow," warned his mother.

"Maybe a jackal has killed our goats," said Devi when she heard that the goats had not been found.

"Don't say that!" said Chitra. "You know what will happen if I have lost the goats."

Chitra dared not think about the consequences of returning home the next day without the goats. He did not sleep that night and as soon as it was light he went out to look for them. He ran through the forest calling them but they did not call back. He went to the river thinking they might be drinking there. He searched the fields in case they were eating the crops. There was no sign of them anywhere. It was nearly midday by the time Chitra returned to the village. Tired and hungry, he walked slowly down the path towards his hut.

"Chitra, Chitra, they have found your goats!" shouted one of his friends.

Chitra felt happy when he heard that the goats had been found. He ran to where his friend was standing.

"Come and see, one is over here," called out his friend. Chitra moved quickly to where a group of people was standing. They moved aside when Chitra came over.

Chitra's heart was pounding. His stomach heaved. Suddenly he knew something was wrong. He looked down, and there was one of his goats lying on the ground covered in blood. The jackal had got her! Chitra ran and hid under a nearby bush. He knew his mother would soon find him. He knew he would get another beating for not looking after the goats.

As he hid trembling in the bush he could hear the other children playing happily nearby. They were laughing and shouting to each other. How he wished he had not played with the other boys. He wished he had not climbed into the trees. He knew it was his job to look after the goats. Losing even one of the goats meant less milk for the family. What would his mother do now? Tears ran down his face as he waited to be punished once again for not doing what he was told to do.

CHAPTER FOUR

WHEN CHITRA was about eighteen years old his cousin Sundar got the opportunity to go to a Christian school in Kathmandu. Every time Sundar came home from school he would tell Chitra all about it and what it was like living in the city.

"It's free to go to my school," Sundar told Chitra one day. "Perhaps next year you could apply and get in too."

"I don't think I will ever get the opportunity to go there. Only a very few boys are accepted," said Chitra. "We have very little money for food, far less for going and living in the city."

"But if you go to my school you wouldn't need to pay the fees," said Sundar. "It's a Christian school and it is free."

"I would love to go there. Perhaps one day I will," replied Chitra sadly.

"As well as teaching us English and other subjects, we learn about Jesus," Sundar told him.

"Who is Jesus?" asked Chitra.

"He is God's son and He died for us. When we believe in Jesus our sins are forgiven," said Sundar.

"My sins can never be forgiven," said Chitra sadly. "I have done so many bad things."

Sundar spent a lot of time with Chitra telling him about Jesus. Chitra listened to what Sundar told him but he didn't believe what he said. There was no way he was going to follow this Jesus!

One day Chitra's grandmother fell ill. She couldn't get up out of her bed.

"Grandmother is very ill," Deu Kumari told the children. "If we don't get her to a doctor she will die." Deu Kumari sat down and began to cry, burying her face in her hands.

"How can we get her to a doctor?" said Devi, starting to cry too. "We have no money for the medicine and it is a long way to go to where the bus is."

"I'll take her," said Chitra, jumping up suddenly.

"How can you take her?" asked Deu Kumari, wiping her eyes with her sari.

"I'll carry her," said Chitra. "I am strong and I will take her to the doctor."

Chitra hurried out of the hut with his mother and sister running after him. When they reached the grandmother's hut Chitra stopped to let his mother go in first. Chitra and Devi waited outside. They could hear the family talking and their grandmother groaning. Then there was the sound of scuffling and furniture being moved.

"What's going on in there?" asked Devi.

"I don't know," said Chitra, peeping in the door to see what was happening.

"Can you see anything?" whispered Devi, standing on her toes to try to see in the door.

"No, I can't see a thing," said Chitra. "It's too dark in there."

At last Deu Kumari came out.

"It has been agreed. You must take Grandmother to the bus and accompany her to see the doctor. She is ready now. Come inside, Chitra."

Chitra entered the dark room. At first he could see nothing. Gradually his eyes got used to the darkness and he saw his grandmother sitting on the edge of the bed. Chitra gently lifted her on to his back.

"This should be enough money to get you to the city and pay for the medicine," said his mother, handing him a small bag.

Chitra didn't ask her where the money had come from. He knew his aunt, who looked after grandmother, must have given all her savings to pay for the medicine.

Chitra went out the door and began the long walk over the hills and through the forest to where they could get a bus to the city. At times he felt he could go no further. He stopped, frequently, to get a breath. His breathing was fast. He was thirsty. His old grandmother hung on to his shoulders.

"We can make it, Chitra," she encouraged. "It's not far now. Just over the next hill."

Chitra looked up at the hill. "It's more like a mountain to me," he gasped, struggling to walk again. After four hours walking they reached the place where the bus would pass. Chitra carefully put his grandmother on the ground beside

Chitra carried his granny through the forest to the hospital

the road. He sat down beside her to wait for the bus to come. Sometime later the bus stopped beside them and Chitra carried his grandmother onto the bus. When they arrived in the city Chitra carried her to the hospital. The doctor was able to give her some medicine. After a few days Chitra and his grandmother started the long journey back home again.

Some months later, while Deu Kumari was cooking the meal, Chitra came running into the hut.

"Mother, Mother," he shouted, "can I go with my friend Keshav to the city tomorrow? He said I could go and stay with him. I can get a job there, and then I can send you some money."

Chitra was now nineteen years old and had done well at school. He still wanted to go to college and train to be a teacher. He knew if he went to the city he could get a job. Then he could earn enough money to pay for his college fees. Now his friend Keshav wanted him to go to the city with him.

"How can you go to the city?" asked Devi. "We have no money, and Mother has no vegetables to sell. You can't walk all the way, it is too far."

"There must be a way," said Chitra. "This might be the only chance I have to go to the city and earn some money for us."

Everyone thought for a while.

Then Deu Kumari said, "I know what to do. I will sell one

of the hens, Chitra. That should pay for the bus fare and a little food. Then you can find a job and buy your own food. You have worked well at school. You are a clever boy. Perhaps one day you will earn enough money to look after your mother and sister too."

"Oh, thank you Mother. I'd better wash my clothes before going to the city," said Chitra, rushing off to the river.

That evening Deu Kumari returned with the money from selling the hen.

"Here is your bus fare and a gift from your uncle," she said, handing Chitra a package. Chitra opened the paper carefully.

"It's a watch!" he exclaimed. "Look everyone, a lovely watch! Now I will not be late for work." Chitra put the watch on his wrist. He looked at it with pride. The only thing he had that was his was his bowl. Now he owned a watch.

"Things are going to be better from now on," Chitra announced.

Chitra had never been to the big city before. Kathmandu was a very strange place. He had not seen the bright lights of the streets, nor the large apartment blocks where many people lived. Everything was very different but Chitra loved the excitement of the city. Everyone was dressed in brightly coloured clothes. Colourful prayer flags fluttered from the buildings. Golden temples shone in the strong sunlight. It was very noisy and dusty in the city. He liked the smell of food coming from the shops along the streets. There was such a variety of food to eat and things for sale. There were so many people milling about, and the roads were full of motorbikes and people. Chitra was amazed by it all.

"How do you like my new motorbike, Chitra?" asked Keshav one evening. "Come on, jump on the back of my bike, and I will take you for a run."

Chitra was terrified. He had never been on a bike before but he didn't want to let his friend know how scared he felt. He climbed carefully on the back of the motorbike and held tightly to Keshav. He shut his eyes as Keshav took off quickly.

When they stopped at a crossroad Keshav turned round and said, "Isn't this great, Chitra?"

Chitra couldn't answer. He was afraid that if he opened his mouth he would be sick. He wished Keshav would stop and let him off. After some time, however, Chitra realised he was not holding on as tightly as before. He was looking at the small market stalls and the large city shops. Even the people on the street fascinated him. He was beginning to enjoy riding on the back of the bike.

It wasn't long before Chitra found a job washing dishes in a restaurant. He stayed with his friend Keshav. As soon as he got his first wage he sent some money home to his mother.

After seven months he got a job in a shoe factory. This job was at night so he decided he could go to college during the day. Sundar's Christian school was far away at the city boundary so he decided to apply to another college near where he lived. This would save the bus fares. He sold his watch to pay for the fees and enrolled for the first term.

As Chitra walked the two miles to college every day he passed many children sleeping rough on the streets. This made him very sad and reminded him of his own poor childhood. His heart went out to these poor children who were helpless, parentless and had no home or anyone to care for them. He began to dream about adopting them and providing schooling for them. This seemed an impossible dream because of the financial difficulties involved.

At first everything went well at college. Then he noticed that no one sat beside him in class.

He was aware that they were talking about him behind his back. One day he overheard one of the boys talking to a friend.

"That Chitra smells! I can't stand the smell of leather and grease," said the boy.

"I know," said his friend. "And just look at his clothes! His trousers are covered in grease. You'd think he would at least wash his trousers and shirt."

"And he fell asleep during the lecture the other day," said the first boy.

"Did he?" replied his friend.

Chitra, not wanting to hear any more, ran off back to his house.

"You're not going to college today?" asked Keshav the next morning.

"Do I smell?" asked Chitra.

"Well, you do a bit," laughed Keshav. "It's the grease from the machines. It gets on your clothes and no matter how often you wash them, the smell and the stain is still there."

Chitra left the room. He went outside and sat down on the steps leading into the apartment.

"I can't go to college if I smell," he said to himself sadly.

From then on Chitra slept during the day and worked in the shoe factory at night. He was very sad and lonely. He hated the work at the factory. The boss was always angry with him. Sometimes he wished he was back home, but he knew he couldn't do that. Returning to his village without passing all his exams would make him a failure. Life, once again, was very hard for Chitra.

CHAPTER FIVE

"CHITRA, CHITRA, wake up! I have some bad news for you," said Keshav, shaking Chitra.

"What is it Keshav?" asked Chitra, jumping out of the bed.

"Your cousin Sundar has been killed in an accident. You have to go to the police station and identify his body. I will come with you. Here, put on your shirt. We have to hurry," said Keshav, handing Chitra his dirty, stained shirt.

Chitra was stunned. He couldn't speak as Keshav pushed him out of the door.

They hurried off to the Police Station. When he saw his cousin's body, Chitra wept. Several other young men were in the room. When Chitra stood up they comforted him and told him that Sundar was now with Jesus.

"Why couldn't Jesus have saved him? Why did he have to die?" cried Chitra angrily. "What good is his faith now?" he wept.

"Come with us to our school. We are taking his body to the church. We are holding the service there. That is what he wanted—a Christian funeral," said one of the young men.

Chitra didn't remember much of what happened after

that. He was too consumed with grief. The following day he sat in the front pew of the church Sundar went to every Sunday. Sundar's friends sat beside him even though he still smelt badly. He listened to Sundar's fellow students singing. Then one man got up and sang a beautiful song that touched Chitra's heart.

"When I die, please don't cry because I will sleep in my Father's lap," he sang. "Thousands of flowers will be on my body and I will be smelling the scent, so do not cry."

He thought of his cousin lying happily in his Father God's lap. He realised that these Christians were happy. They were saying that Sundar was now at peace with Jesus. They were praising the one true God for Sundar, not chanting prayers to one of the 33 million Hindu gods.

That night Chitra couldn't sleep. He kept hearing Sundar's voice telling him about this Jesus whom he loved. The music sung in the church played in his head. He was angry. He was sad. Nothing seemed to make sense. Sundar's Christian friends were so different from the people he knew. They were kind and helpful. They didn't keep away from him. In fact the preacher had sat beside him and put his hand on his shoulder. He felt loved and cared for, for the first time in his life.

"But why did Jesus let Sundar die? If God loved Sundar, why did He not save him?" Chitra asked himself over and over again.

Suddenly, as the dawn broke through the curtains of his room, Chitra was aware of a very bright light shining all round the room. He was startled by a vision of his cousin standing in front of him clothed in white.

"Sundar!" Chitra shouted out. "Sundar, is that you?"

The door opened and Sundar's friends came rushing in.

"What's wrong, Chitra? We heard you shouting out. Are you all right?"

"I saw my cousin standing right here! He was smiling at me."

"You see, your cousin is happy. Sundar is with Jesus in heaven," said one of the friends, sitting on the bed beside Chitra.

"Why couldn't Jesus save Sundar? He was a good man. He was one of Jesus' followers, wasn't he? So why did Jesus not save him?"

"Jesus *did* save Sundar," said the friend. "Sundar has eternal life and will live forever in Heaven with Jesus. All his fears and worries are gone now. He is at peace."

The two men sat on the bed. Neither spoke for some time. Then Sundar's friend said:

"You can be a follower of Jesus too, if you believe."

"I am afraid to believe. My people will disown me. I will be thrown out of the village. My mother will not speak to me," said Chitra sadly. "I have caused her enough trouble. For me to become a Christian would kill her. No, I can't believe all this nonsense."

After the funeral Chitra returned home to his family. The whole village went into mourning for Sundar. It was so different from the way the Christians had acted. Chitra spent many days quietly thinking over all the events that had happened.

"What's the matter with Chitra?" Devi asked her mother one day. "He is very quiet and has hardly spoken a word since Sundar's death."

"He was very fond of Sundar. They were good friends," replied her mother. "I think he is just missing him. He will soon get over it. Life has to go on."

"I think it has something to do with the Christians at Sundar's school. Maybe Chitra has become a Christian too," said Devi.

"He had better not!" Deu Kumari exclaimed. "He has to look after me in my old age. He has to pray to the spirits or I will never rest at peace when I die. He can't become a Christian." With that she walked out of the hut angrily.

On the bus back to Kathmandu a few days later Chitra was thinking about Jesus. Suddenly he began to cry again. He was overwhelmed by a great sense of peace. Then he *knew* that God was real. Somehow he had to find out more about this Jesus and the Christian faith. He dried his eyes, wiped his dirty face and made the decision to find a church as soon as he could.

Two weeks later Chitra found a group of Christians who met in one of the believers' homes. Chitra decided to become a Christian and follow Jesus! Shortly after his baptism Chitra was so excited about his new-found faith that he decided to go back to his village and tell all his friends and family about Jesus.

For two days Chitra taught his fellow villagers about Jesus and how He died so that they could be forgiven. All their sins could be wiped out and they would go to Heaven when they died, he told them.

"All my sins have been forgiven," Chitra said. "You all know how bad I was. Your sins can be forgiven too."

They listened to what he was saying and welcomed him back into their community. Then disaster struck. Devi came running down the village street shouting:

"Come quickly, everyone! A tiger has attacked our flock of goats. Some of the men have chased it away. Everyone is very afraid."

Chitra came hurrying out of the hut.

"Come quickly Chitra, we don't know what to do," Devi told him.

Chitra and some friends had been talking together inside their hut when Devi arrived with the news of the tiger. So they followed Devi to where the tiger had killed one of the goats.

"What happened?" asked Chitra, gasping for breath after running all the way.

"Just as well we were near here or the tiger would have got more of the goats," said one of the villagers. "I managed to scare it away and shouted for the others who were in the next field."

"Did you see the tiger?" asked Devi who always liked a bit of excitement.

"Yes," answered the man. "It gave me such a fright!"

"We haven't seen a tiger in these parts for years. I wonder why it came here?" said another older villager.

The people returned to their homes, afraid now that a tiger was in the area.

"Perhaps it will come back tonight," said Devi.

"You always think the worst," said her mother, shutting the door behind her. "But we will keep the goats in the hut tonight just in case."

"What are the goats doing in the hut?" asked Chitra when he came home later that night.

"Mother is afraid the tiger will come back tonight and eat us all up!" said Devi with a laugh.

"It's no laughing matter," warned her mother, shooing the goats to the back of the hut.

"We don't need to be afraid," said Chitra. "God will look after us. He will keep us safe."

The following day Devi was out in the village buying some food. She noticed some of the village men standing in the street talking together. When she came up to where they were, they stopped talking and moved away. As Devi returned to her hut later she noticed the men talking together again and there seemed to be more of them now.

"There is a big meeting going on up there," said Devi as she met her mother in the street.

"Maybe they are going out to catch the tiger," said her mother.

"I wish I was a boy, and then I could go with them," said Devi.

"Don't be silly, tiger hunting is no fun, I can assure you," replied Deu Kumari, rubbing her back. "Here, help me carry this bag of food. My back is aching. Where's that brother of yours? He is never here when you need him."

"He is probably talking to the men about Jesus. He certainly seems to believe in all that nonsense. What do you think about it Mother?" asked Devi.

"I don't believe it and Chitra will soon change his mind. Come on, we have no time to think about these things. Too much to do just to feed and clothe ourselves," said Deu Kumari as they arrived at their hut.

Devi and her mother prepared the meal outside their hut. Then Deu Kumari stopped what she was doing and stood up.

"Listen, what is all that noise about?" she said looking up the village street. Devi looked up too. "Sounds like men shouting. Let's go and see what's going on. Perhaps the tiger has come back," said Devi excitedly. She handed her mother the basket with the maize she had been cleaning. Then she ran up the street.

"It sounds like an angry mob," said Deu Kumari, putting down the basket. She hurried after Devi.

The noise got louder as they reached the end of the street. Crowds of people were shouting and running down the street out of the village. Devi and Deu Kumari followed the crowd, unaware of what was happening.

"It's Chitra," said a woman standing in the shop door as they passed by. "They're throwing him out of the village because of all his preaching about Jesus. It's because of him that the tiger has attacked our village!" she shouted after them.

Deu Kumari hurried on, afraid because of what she had just heard. Devi was no longer excited about a tiger hunt. She was afraid for her brother. It was difficult for Deu Kumari to push her way through the people. She was out of breath with running.

"You go on, Devi, and see what is happening. I can't go any further. I'll stay here and rest," said Deu Kumari, stopping by the roadside.

"Will you be all right?" asked Devi.

"Yes, yes. You run on and try to stop them. Oh, what is going to happen to us now?" she cried.

Devi pushed her way through the angry crowd. These were her friends, people she had known for a long time. In this crowd were neighbours who had helped them in their time of need.

"Perhaps the old woman was wrong. Maybe this has nothing to do with Chitra," she said to herself as she squeezed through between the people. At last she reached the front of the crowd. Angry men were shaking their fists and shouting loudly. She couldn't see Chitra.

"What's going on?" she cried. Then she saw Chitra. Her brother was trying to talk to the men. They were shoving him away and shouting at him. Devi ran up to her brother.

"What's happening?" she cried. She turned towards the crowd. "What are you doing? Chitra has done you no harm. Leave him alone!" Devi fell at Chitra's feet crying. The crowd stopped and moved away.

"We don't want him back in our village," said one of the men.

"It was his fault the tiger came here. This is an evil omen. The spirits are angry with Chitra talking about Jesus," said another.

"The spirits have sent the tiger to warn us," said one of the village elders.

"Leave us alone. We don't want to hear about this Jesus. You go back to the city!" shouted a neighbour.

Devi sat on the ground crying. Slowly the crowd left.

Chitra sat down beside his sister. "Don't cry, Devi," he said. "Everything will be all right. Our village is not ready for Jesus yet. I'm leaving. Take care of our mother. I will send you some money when I can. I am going back to the church and college. If you can, come to the city to visit me. Now go back to Mother. I will walk to Kathmandu. I have friends there who will look after me. Don't worry; remember I have Jesus keeping me safe."

"Oh, Chitra, what will happen to us? I am afraid for you but I know you are strong and you believe in this Jesus. Take care."

Chitra and Devi said goodbye. Devi walked slowly back to her village wondering how her friends and neighbours could do this to her brother. Chitra began his journey back to the church, his studies, and his Christian friends.

There was a spare room in the house-church, so Chitra was allowed to stay there. He got a better job in a tobacconist's shop which paid him good money. This money enabled him to return to college. He was no longer smelly. His clothes were clean and had no grease on them. But Chitra never forgot the poor street children and prayed about his vision. He also shared his concerns about these children with his fellow believers. They too prayed for an answer to their prayer for these children.

Chitra studied for three years and got his certificate as a teacher. During all this time he was able to send some money back home to his mother.

CHAPTER SIX

CHITRA WAS SWEEPING the floor in the church one day, singing away to himself as he usually did. The Pastor came in and stopped to listen.

"You have a lovely voice, Chitra," said the Pastor. "You must join our choir."

"I love singing," said Chitra. "Even when I was a little boy I used to sing while I did my chores. Now I can't stop singing all the new hymns I am learning."

"What was the song you were singing just now?" asked the Pastor. "I don't think I know it."

"I have just made it up in my head," replied Chitra. "It happens quite a lot. Suddenly a tune will come into my mind and I think up the words to go with it."

"You have been given this gift by God," said the Pastor. "Make sure you use it wisely."

In 1997 another wonderful thing happened to change Chitra's life forever.

"I have a job in England!" Chitra announced to his Pastor. "Some friends in England have sent me a ticket to fly to London and there is a job at Scargall, a Christian guest house. I will be washing dishes and taking care of the guests there."

"I knew God had a plan for you but I didn't think it would involve going to England," replied the Pastor in surprise.

"I will be able to learn to speak English," said Chitra excitedly. "Then I can read books about Jesus and the Christian faith."

"Will you come back to Nepal, Chitra?" asked the Pastor.

"Of course I will," said Chitra. "I am sure God's plan is for me to work here in my own village. One day we will build our own church."

"That is a very big vision," said the Pastor, "but with God nothing is impossible. We will be praying for you, Chitra. God bless you as you go on this amazing journey."

Chitra did well in England. He made many friends. One of the guests noticed his beautiful singing voice and encouraged him with his music. Sometime later Chitra was invited to go to Iona, a sacred island with a famous Abbey, off the west coast of Scotland. There he met the Rev. John Bell, who suggested that Chitra should go to Glasgow to study Theology at the International Christian College. Chitra didn't know how this could happen. He returned to Scargall and worked a further ten months before going back to Nepal.

Back in his home church Chitra again called the Deacons and Pastor to pray seriously about starting up a home for orphans which he had been dreaming about. Every Sunday they fasted and prayed for guidance from the Lord. The time was not right, however, but they continued to pray about it. Chitra also discussed with his mother and his Pastor the possibility of further study in Scotland.

As soon as he told his mother about his desire to return to the United Kingdom, she told him:

"You will have to get married first. We can't have you going off to a foreign land not married. You may marry a girl in Scotland and then you will never come back to Nepal."

"Yes, better get you married," laughed Devi, "then you won't be so quick to run off to other countries!"

"I can't get married; I have too much to do. I need to pray and think about how I am going to manage to study in Scotland," said Chitra who had not even thought about marriage.

Chitra knew it was no use arguing with his mother. If she had made up her mind about something nothing would make her change it.

"My friend from the next village has a lovely daughter, Sharda. You know her. Do you like her?" asked his mother.

"Yes, I know her and I like her, but she is too young. How can you arrange a marriage?" he asked.

"Just be here tomorrow," smiled Deu Kumari as Chitra left the hut.

Chitra decided he would meet Sharda whom he knew was a Christian too. So the following day he went with his mother on the bus to Sharda's village.

Deu Kumari managed to find a seat inside the crowded bus, but there was no seat for Chitra. It was cooler riding on the outside, so Chitra happily hung onto the side of the bus. He felt quite excited as he held onto the open window.

"Oh God, please let me know if this is the right thing to

do, and that Sharda is the right one for me," Chitra prayed as the bus bumped over the rough road sending dust flying into the air.

Chitra's heart began to beat very fast when they arrived at the village main street. As they went into the house church Chitra began to feel anxious. The Pastor would be there with the young girl. He had never thought about being married. He had been too busy working in the fields, then learning about God to think about girls. Still, he knew this was what his mother wanted. In his village this was what was expected. It was not considered right for a young man to be on his own; he had to find a wife sometime.

"Hello Chitra," said the Pastor. "I would like you to meet Sharda."

Chitra felt really pleased when he was introduced to Sharda. He had noticed Sharda in church and she had noticed him.

In 1999 Sharda and Chitra were married in the house church. It was a very happy day. After the wedding they went back to Chitra's village and lived with his mother and sister. Chitra worked there growing rice, maize and dhido.[2]

"I will help you in your work," said Sharda, "and I will look after your mother too."

A year later Sharda had a baby girl, Mahima. About the same time Deu Kumari and Devi became Christians too. Shortly after this Chitra got a letter telling him there was a place for him at the International Christian College in

2. A type of grain grown in the mountainous regions of Nepal which can be made into a kind of thick porridge.

Glasgow. Chitra was very excited that God had answered his prayers. He discussed with Sharda the possibility of going to Scotland.

"You must accept this opportunity that God has given you, Chitra," said Sharda. "I will be fine here with your mother and sister. They will help me with the baby and I will care for your mother."

So Chitra accepted the place at ICC. When all the arrangements had been made, Chitra left for College in Scotland.

In 2001 Sharda and Mahima joined Chitra in Scotland and they found a flat in Glasgow. Sharda cooked for Chitra and looked after Mahima.

One day Chitra got a letter from his Pastor.

"It's bad news, Sharda," said Chitra, passing the letter to his wife.

"How could he do this?" asked Sharda after she had read the letter.

"Well, it is his house, so I suppose he can do what he likes with it now," replied Chitra.

The house where his little church met was no longer available. The man who owned it had died and his son wanted the house for himself. The church would have to find somewhere else to worship.

"Come Sharda, we will need to ask God about this," said Chitra, getting on his knees.

Chitra and Sharda prayed for an answer to their problem.

While they were praying Chitra was given the vision of a new church building. He decided that somehow they would build a church belonging to the believers where they could worship freely.

CHAPTER SEVEN

THE NEXT DAY, during lunch, Chitra told a few of his fellow students about his church in Kathmandu having no place to worship. He shared with them about his vision to build their own church.

"It will cost us £3000 to buy some land and put up a building that we can use to worship in," Chitra told them.

"How can it cost so little?" asked Tricia, one of the students.

"Sterling goes a long way in Nepal," replied Chitra. "£1 is equal to 125NPR in our money. We can buy a lot with that amount. I have been in touch with my Pastor and he says we can purchase some land on the outskirts of Kathmandu. We will build the church ourselves."

After Chitra left the dining hall the others began to discuss what Chitra had just shared with them.

"Imagine Chitra wanting to build a church! He has no money, nothing," said Tricia to Anne, another of the students.

"I know," said Anne. "He came here with nothing and he has no job."

"I'm amazed at his vision. How could one young man raise £3000 to build a church?" said Tricia as they walked back to their class.

"What faith these foreign students have," thought Tricia to herself.

That evening Tricia was at her local church Prayer Meeting.

"I was talking with one of my fellow students at lunchtime today and was really amazed at the vision he has," Tricia told them. "Can I share it with you?" she asked.

The group was always interested in what was going on at ICC and enjoyed the stories Tricia brought to the Prayer Meeting about life in the Christian College.

"What exciting thing are you going to share with us?" asked Patrick, an elder in the church and leader of the Prayer Meeting.

"Well, this young lad Chitra, who is from Nepal, wants to build his own church," began Tricia. "The group he worshiped with in Nepal met in one of the believers' homes. This man has died and his son wants the house for himself. Now they have nowhere to meet. The interesting thing is that it will only cost them £3000 to buy the land and build their church."

"£3000 is not much money to build a church when you think about it," said Patrick. "We will pray about this tonight. I am sure if it is God's plan for this little group of Christians in Nepal to have their own church building, then something will happen to bring this about."

Unknown to Chitra, Tricia or Patrick, God was indeed working this out. He had a plan for the Christian Church in Nepal. God had called Chitra to share in spreading the Good News and He was equipping him and His church for this task.

At an elder's meeting the following day the minister, Rev. John, stood up.

"I have some good news to share with you tonight," he announced. "A substantial sum of money has been left to our church. I know there is much work needing to be done in the church and to our halls. But before we decide how to spend this money wisely, I think it should be tithed. I would like to give a tenth of the total money to God's work elsewhere in the world."

The elders talked about this for some time. One man thought it should go to the fabric committee. Others thought it should be spent on the children, providing much needed material for the youth work. In the end, however, it was agreed that a tenth should go to mission.

"Has anyone got an idea of where this money is needed?" asked Rev. John.

Patrick knew immediately and said, "At the Prayer Meeting last night we heard about a young man from Nepal who needs just £3000 to build a church. They need the money to buy some land, then they will put up a building they can use to worship in."

Amazingly by the end of the Session Meeting it was agreed to give some of the money to Chitra.

Other people in Britain heard about Chitra's vision and they also gave some money. When Chitra completed his two years at ICC he left with a degree in Theology and the £3000 he needed to build his church!

Chitra returned to Nepal with Sharda and Mahima. Their Pastor bought the land and the congregation built the church.

A Church building of their own to worship in

Chitra's vision didn't end there. The Church agreed to start the orphan's home and bought a couple of children's beds. They also bought plastic containers which they gave to each member of the Church. The idea was to separate one handful of their rice and put it in the container. They named the plastic containers *'Grace Boxes'*. Thus each week the Church was able to collect 30 kg. of rice for the orphans. Then Chitra and his wife adopted three orphaned children. At the next Church meeting they discussed how to run the children's home and what would be a good name for it. One of the Church's members suggested the name 'Grace Children's home' as the children would be supported by the Grace Boxes. So that was the new name given to the home for orphans which Chitra had dreamed about all those years before. It was felt that the Home should be legalized so it was registered with the Government in 2005 as a charity.

Later on they had to build a bigger house to accommodate ten more orphaned children who came to live in their home. Sharda cared for these children as well as her own three. Dollar Parish Church in Scotland pledged to send money each year to help with the clothing and education of these children. Many other churches and Christian groups also donated to the work of spreading the Good News to the people of Nepal. Some years later several sister churches were built in the neighbouring villages and many believers were baptised.

CHAPTER EIGHT

"I'M SURE there is water here," said Chitra to Sharda one day as he was walking across the compound where the Church and children's home had been built.

"If you think there is, why not try digging for a well?" replied Sharda. "You know how difficult it is to fetch water every day."

"Wouldn't it be wonderful if people from the surrounding area came to us for water?" said Chitra excitedly.

"We must pray about it," said Sharda. "I'm sure God will show you where the well should be dug."

At the next meeting of the Church, Chitra told his fellow believers about his vision of a well built in their compound. Everyone was very excited. They prayed and fasted for several weeks, then began to dig the well.

"Look at that!" said Chitra proudly several weeks later. He was standing by the new well.

The children were splashing themselves with the water Sharda had drawn from the well. Even the old men were throwing water over each other. Everyone was happy that God had provided water for them right in the middle of where they lived.

"We must thank Almighty God for the provision of this well," said Chitra that night as the little group of Christians gathered round the well to bless it.

"This will be a real blessing to all who come here for water," announced the Pastor. "We will share this with anyone in need. That will be a good example to our neighbours who still follow the Hindu gods."

God was not finished with Chitra yet. He still had much more for him to do. Another project that Chitra completed was a CD of Christian music that could be used in worship in the new churches. Chitra made up many new songs and recorded the CD at a studio in Kathmandu. He called his CD "Struggle". He sent copies of the CD to the UK as well as to other Christian groups in Nepal to raise money for Grace Children's Home for orphans.

"Come quickly!" shouted Chitra's uncle one day. "She's trying to jump into the fire again."

Chitra had been visiting his uncle in the village where he grew up. His uncle had asked Chitra if he could help his wife who went crazy sometimes and tried to sit on the fire. Everyone in the village knew she was possessed by an evil spirit. They were afraid of these evil spirits. Nothing seemed to help. No one could get rid of this evil.

Chitra looked at his aunt dancing round the fire in a frenzy. He looked at the villagers and saw their frightened faces.

"Jesus can help her," he said to them. "Do you want me to ask Jesus to heal her?"

"Yes, if Jesus can heal her we will believe and listen to all you have been telling us about Jesus," said his uncle anxiously. "Please help her. She will kill herself if something is not done for her."

Just at that moment Chitra's aunt jumped into the fire. She sat down on the flames seemingly unaware of the fire burning her sari.

Chitra prayed, took her by the hand and pulled her from the fire. He placed his hands on her and prayed again. Immediately she stopped jumping about. She stood quietly beside Chitra. Then she began to shake violently and fell to the ground.

"She's dead!" shouted one of the villagers.

"What have you done to her?" shouted another man.

Chitra continued to pray and kept his hand on her. Suddenly she sat up. She looked about her.

"What happened?" she asked.

"Are you all right?" asked her husband, rushing over to her.

"Yes, I feel fine," she said, getting to her feet. God had completely healed her. She was free from the evil spirits and the burns on her legs.

"We believe that your God is all powerful," said his uncle in amazement.

"I want to be a follower of this God of yours too," said one of the villagers.

Chitra stayed in the village for 12 days explaining to them about salvation through belief in Jesus. He told them he would come back the following month with the Pastor to baptise anyone who wanted to become a Christian. The villagers, who had thrown Chitra out of his village because of his belief in Jesus, now wanted to be Christians too!

"I want to build a school for my village," Chitra told Sharda one night after he got back from visiting his uncle in his old village.

"You and your visions!" said Sharda with a laugh. "How can you build a school there? We have no money. All we get is needed to feed and educate the children. There is nothing extra."

"I know. I know we have very little as it is," said Chitra sadly, "but I am sure God has given me this new vision. If this is from Him, we will build a school in my village."

Sometime later a letter came from Scotland. It was an invitation to go to Glasgow to celebrate a friend's birthday. Along with the letter was the money for the fare.

"How can I go?" said Chitra sadly. "The money for the ticket could be spent here. No, I don't think I can go."

"There is always a way if this is what God wants," said his mother. "You are always telling us this, Chitra. If you have to go to Scotland then God will provide."

"I have too much to do here. I want to start building the school in our village."

"Perhaps this is God's answer to your prayer for funds to build this school," said Sharda. "If you go to the UK you will meet all the people you know. Tell them about the vision for a school in your old village. I am sure God will move their hearts as He has done before."

"Maybe," said Chitra sadly. "But it is a lot of money to spend on the ticket. It might be better spent here."

Chitra was torn between his desire to return to the UK or to stay and work in his village.

"We will have to get started soon or we won't have the building finished before the rains come," said Chitra's uncle.

"I know, but if I go to the UK, can you get the others in the village to work on the school while I am away?" Chitra asked, looking at the piece of land the villagers had cleared for the school.

"Of course I can," replied his uncle. "You know how happy they are with the idea of their own school. You go to the UK and bring back the money we need for the roof. We can make the bricks and plaster the walls, but we can't pay for the tin for the roof."

"I suppose I could go," said Chitra. "I have many friends. When they hear about the school, I am sure they will want to help."

"This is God's answer to our prayers. How else could we afford to put the roof on the building?" asked his uncle.

Chitra did go to the UK. He went to the celebration for his friend's birthday. He met many of his old friends and spoke at many meetings. When he returned to Nepal he not only had the money for the school roof, he had a digital camera as well. Now he could send photos to his friends in the UK. He wanted to share with them the wonderful answers to prayer God had given him.

God used one small boy who had nothing, to achieve

amazing things. He enabled Chitra not only to build a church, but also to build a new children's home so that they wouldn't have to pay rent for a house. In Grace Children's Home unloved and deprived orphans will find love and security. With God's help and power they have also built Marion School and three daughter churches in the surrounding area.

In 2012, four years after the church had been built in the village where Chitra was born, 14 people were baptised. This took the total to 80 believers baptised from Chitra's village.

The children enjoy learning and playing at their school

Another miracle happened when God gave Chitra the opportunity to meet the Prime Minister of Nepal. As a board member of the government school which Chitra attended as a poor boy with no shoes and no proper clothes, Chitra was invited to the special Golden Jubilee celebration. The Prime Minister had to come by helicopter to visit such a remote village for the celebrations. As they sat together Chitra was able to talk to him and discuss the needs of the village. Chitra handed the Prime Minister an appeal letter on behalf of the villagers, requesting clean drinking water for the village, a health project and a new building to be constructed for Marion School.

From a few Christian believers the church has grown so much that they have had to knock down the east side of the old church building to make it bigger. God has brought many people to the church. This bigger building can hold 300 people. Seventy per cent of the funding has been raised by the local congregation. The Christians in Nepal still need our support and prayers but it is truly amazing just what God can do when one person answers the call to fulfil God's vision for His church to His Glory.

Grace Children's Home for orphans

The congregation gather for worship

The hiding place among the banana trees

No Shoes

CHAPTER ONE

THE EMPTY HUT

"QUICK, HIDE IN HERE!" shouted Alice to Julius, Constance, Kenneth and Rozettie, as she pushed her children under the banana trees. "We'll be safe here tonight."

"We can't sleep out here in the jungle!" said Kenneth in alarm. "The wild animals will eat us."

"God will keep us safe," said their mother. Alice pulled some large leaves from a nearby banana tree. "Here, put these banana leaves on the ground, we can lie on them."

Alice laid the leaves on the ground and the children sat down on them. Rozettie began to cry.

"Why did Dad throw us out of the hut again?" she asked between her sobs.

"He's not well," was all her mother could say.

"Drunk, more like," said Kenneth in disgust. "I saw him in the village at the shops with his friends. They were all drinking and laughing and making an awful noise."

"Dad has been having trouble at work," said Alice. "He'll be all right soon. We can sell a few things that we don't need. Then he can pay off his debts and we will be as we were before all this trouble happened," assured their mother.

The children huddled close together on the banana leaves. They were afraid to go to sleep as they lay listening to the noises in the jungle.

"Is that a lion roaring in the distance?" asked Rozettie who had only just stopped crying.

"Don't be silly," said Kenneth. "Lions don't roam about here, they live in the Game Park."

"No, it's not a lion, Rozettie. It may be a wild dog or a hyena, but it is far away," her mother said convincingly. "Now go to sleep and I'll watch out that no wild animals come near us."

"But you need to sleep too," said Kenneth, who knew that his mother had to work in the garden to make sure that there was some food for them to eat.

"I'll be all right. You get some sleep, you have school in the morning," replied Alice. "You are a bright boy, Kenneth. You need to work hard at school and pass all the exams. Then you can get a good job."

The thought of school helped Kenneth take his mind off the frightening situation they were in. He liked school. His teacher was very pleased with him and had told him that next year he could go on to the senior school if he passed his exams.

He lay down and tried to sleep. His eyes were tired and soon closed.

"Did you sleep last night, Kenneth?" asked Rozettie as they walked to school the next day.

"Yes I did," replied Kenneth. "I didn't think I would. I was really scared staying out there all night, but I must have been tired as I fell asleep as soon as I closed my eyes."

"I didn't think I would be able to sleep either, but I did. Maybe God did look after us as Mum said," replied Rozettie.

It took the children longer to walk back to their village from their hiding place. Kenneth knew that classes would have started by the time they reached the school.

"You're late," scolded the teacher as Kenneth sat down in his seat.

No one said a word. Kenneth didn't want anyone to know they had slept out in the bush last night because their father had thrown them out of their hut.

After school the children wondered if it was safe to go home. Would their father be in the hut? Would he be angry and shout at them? Was he arguing and quarrelling with their mother? The children crept round the back of the hut. They saw their mother in the garden pulling up the weeds between the maize. She stopped what she was doing when she saw the children.

"It's all right," she shouted over to them. "Come on in, your father is not here, he left some time ago."

The children ran up to their mother and she hugged them tightly. There were tears in her eyes as she told them their father had decided to go to the city to try to get some work.

For the next few weeks everything went well. There were

plenty of vegetables growing in their garden. Alice cooked some for their evening meals and sold the rest at the local market. The children went to school each day. After school the older children helped some neighbours by collecting wood for the fire or sweeping their yard. This gave them a little money to buy some milk. They were also able to buy some soap to wash their clothes.

One day the children arrived at school as usual. The teacher met them at the door.

"Sorry, children, you can't come into class today. Your school fees have not been paid for some time now and we have decided you will have to stay at home till your father has enough money to pay us."

The children could not believe what they had just heard! Rozettie began to cry. Kenneth took her hand and walked back out of the school yard. All the other pupils went into their classrooms. Only Kenneth and his brother and sisters didn't go in. They walked slowly across the road to their hut.

"What's the matter?" asked Alice as they came into the garden. "Why are you not in school?"

"They won't let us!" shouted Kenneth, close to tears. "Dad hasn't paid the fees."

"What? He's not paid the fees? But I gave him some money to pay the fees before he left," said their mother angrily.

"He probably spent it in the pub before he went," said Kenneth. "What are we going to do now?"

"I don't know what to do. We have no money and your

father is away looking for work in the city. I haven't heard from him since he left. He hasn't sent us any money as he promised," said their mother. She turned away bending down to pick some maize as she didn't want to let her children see her crying. The children went into the hut and sat down on the bed.

"Well, at least we still have our beds," said Julius, the eldest boy in the family, as he looked about the empty room. There were no table or chairs now as they had been sold weeks ago to buy some food. The rug had gone, the set of drawers had gone and even some of their clothes had been sold.

"No use sitting here feeling sorry for ourselves," said Kenneth, jumping off the bed, "come on, we need to get some money."

"I suppose now that we can't go to school we can get some work in the village," said Julius hopefully.

"But what can I do?" said Rozettie, starting to cry.

"You can help Mum in the garden," said Constance, her big sister. "She needs help picking the maize, then you can go with her to sell it at the market."

The children tried to cheer each other up but they were very sad at not being allowed to go to school. Kenneth, especially, was sad and angry.

"I'll not be able to sit the exams this term and I'll not get to secondary school," he said as the children went to tell their mother what they planned to do.

"I hate Dad," he added, "it's his fault we are in such a state."

"Oh, don't say that, Kenneth," said Constance hopefully. "Things will work out in the end I'm sure."

Things didn't get any better. The children could hear the others in the school yard. They watched them go into their classes. They ran away and hid when the teacher went past their hut. None of their friends spoke to them now, and to make matters worse, their father, Charles, had returned from the city drunk as usual with no money and no job.

"Stay away from the hut today," warned their mother, "your father is in a rage!"

"I'll bet you he has no money for drink," said Kenneth angrily. "That will be why he has come back home to see if we have any money for him."

Although his brother and sisters were angry with their father too, it was Kenneth who seemed to show his disapproval the most. He had the most to lose by not going to school, so he felt his father had let him down. Kenneth felt utterly rejected by his father, his friends and his teacher. Later that night the children crept into the hut to get a blanket.

"Get out, get out!" shouted Charles.

They knew they would be sleeping in the jungle again. This happened every time their father got drunk. When he was not drinking, life was good. He was kind and talked with the children. When he had some money, however, he would go to the village for a drink. Then, when he came home drunk, he would throw them out of the hut. Many nights were spent out in the open under the banana trees.

"I don't like sleeping out here in the jungle," said Rozettie when they reached their hideout.

"We have been safe so far, Rozettie," said her mother. "Your dad won't find us here and he will be asleep when we get back in the morning."

"These mosquitoes are biting my legs," complained Constance, waving a leaf above her head to keep the mosquitoes away.

"It never used to be like this," grumbled Kenneth, lying on his back. He looked up into the sky. "Do you remember Dad telling us that God made all these stars?" he asked his mother.

"Dad even knew the names of some of them," said Constance, looking up at the stars twinkling in the dark blue of the night sky.

"That seems such a long time ago," said their mother sadly. "We were happy then. Your father would go to church every Sunday and teach at the fellowship group. I don't know what has got into him. I don't understand why he needs to drink so much beer. We have nothing left now. The maize is all sold and the vegetables won't be ready for a few weeks yet. I don't know what to do. If it wasn't for you, Kenneth, and your brother and sisters working to bring me a little money, we would starve."

Kenneth moved nearer his mother and put his arm round her shoulder.

"Don't cry Mum," Kenneth said comfortingly, "something will happen to get us all back to how we used to be. I can work and so can Julius and Constance. We will manage."

But he knew deep down in his heart that things were very bad. It was hard to get any work. He was sad when he saw the other children go to school. He felt hungry all the time.

"How can things get any better?" he wondered to himself.

The next day the family went back to their hut. Alice opened the door carefully not wanting to disturb her husband. She gasped in horror as she went into the room. It was empty.

"Even the beds are gone!" cried Rozettie as she followed her mother into the hut.

"That's it!" said Kenneth in a determined voice, "I am going to find him."

"Don't be foolish," said his mother sadly, "you can't do anything. He's probably sold the beds for drink." She went out to the garden and began to hoe round the vegetables.

The children looked about their empty hut. They couldn't believe nearly everything was gone.

CHAPTER TWO

A CHANGE IN KENNETH

"THERE'S A NEW SPEAKER coming to the fellowship tomorrow, Kenneth," said his mother one day. "The Pastor wants you to play your drum at the service."

"I can't go looking like this," said Kenneth, pointing to his torn shirt and dirty trousers, "and I haven't got any shoes. What will people think of me in this state? The children laugh at me all the time because I have no shoes," he added.

"Never mind what you look like," said Julius, "no one will see you at the back of the church anyway."

"You can keep your feet hidden behind the drum," laughed Constance. "You are good at playing the drum and the Pastor has asked you to play, so you had better go."

"I'll think about it," answered Kenneth sullenly.

"Just as well you keep your drum at the church or you wouldn't have it now," said Rozettie sadly.

She was the youngest and couldn't remember what it had been like before their dad spent all their money. Kenneth had told her that their father used to have his own business.

The family also used to have a large plot of land before their father sold it. Rozettie remembered nothing of this. All she knew was her father shouting at them and quarrelling with their mother. She only knew a half-empty hut with little food. She had never had a pair of shoes. Her sister's shoes had worn out before they fitted her. Rozettie just kept close to her mother and did what she was told. That way she kept out of trouble. On the other hand Kenneth seemed to be in trouble all the time. He was angry and aggressive and argued with his father. He often had to run and hide from his father. Life was very hard for the family.

"Are you going to play your drum?" Rozettie asked Kenneth the next day as they helped their mother in the garden.

"I might," Kenneth answered. His mother looked up from weeding the vegetables.

"I think you should go," she said. "Perhaps the singing will make you feel better."

Alice knew her son was very sad. She knew he longed to go to school, and worried about his behaviour, but there was nothing she could do to help except pray for him.

When the vegetables had been picked and put in the basket, the children ran off to the river to wash their hands and feet. They hurried back to the hut, then went with their mother to the church. Kenneth decided to go too. He sat at the back of the church and played his drum as the people came in, but he hid behind the door so that no one could see him. As Kenneth watched his fingers beat out the rhythm he noticed his dirty trousers. He shut his eyes so that he couldn't see the mess he was in. He listened to the music as he played his drum, and his whole body began to sway in time to the music.

Kenneth plays his drum

He started to sing and his heart felt glad. When the lady preacher got up to speak he listened carefully to what she was saying. At the end of her talk she invited anyone to come forward and give their lives to Christ. Kenneth watched as several people got up out of their seats and moved towards the front of the church. He saw the Pastor and the elders praying for each of them.

Suddenly Kenneth found himself walking down the aisle to the front of the church, his bare feet taking him towards the Pastor. His heart was pounding in his chest and his hands began to sweat.

"What if Jesus rejects me?" he thought to himself as he reached the front.

The lady preacher came up to him and put her hand on his shoulder.

"God loves you," she said, "Jesus died for you. Do you want to be one of Jesus' followers?"

Kenneth knelt at her feet and asked, "Does Jesus really want me?" Tears were streaming down his dirty face as he looked up at the Pastor and the lady.

"Of course Jesus wants you," replied the lady preacher with a smile. "Jesus loves everyone and He wants them to be His friend."

"You know this, Kenneth," the Pastor said, "but you have to decide for yourself."

"I want to follow Jesus and have Him live in my heart," answered Kenneth. "I am sorry for all the bad things I have done. I need Jesus to help me live as I should."

As the Pastor and the lady prayed for him, Kenneth was aware of a wonderful feeling welling up inside him. He felt the love of Jesus coming to him and making him clean. When he stood up he felt his face break into a smile. Kenneth had not smiled for a long, long time. Now he was smiling and jumping for joy. Jesus had found him—a twelve-year-old boy! He joined in the singing and sang with all his heart. He prayed to God, "Thank you Jesus for saving me! I will follow you for the rest of my life. I will do what you want. Help me, Jesus."

However, the next day Kenneth was very angry with his father as usual. He was about to challenge his father when something stopped him. It was like a voice was speaking to him. He knew it was God telling him to love his father. Kenneth stopped what he was doing and ran outside the hut. He needed to think.

"You want me to love my father?" he said out loud. "Jesus, you want me to love my father who has sold all our things and gets drunk?" he asked again.

Kenneth sat down on the road and lent against the wall by his hut. He thought over what he had just felt in his heart. He needed to talk to someone about this. He decided to go and talk to the Pastor, so he ran over to the church.

"Pastor, Pastor, Jesus has just spoken to me," he blurted out quickly when he found the Pastor.

"Take a breath, Kenneth, and tell me all about it," said the Pastor, leading Kenneth to a seat in the church.

"Well," began Kenneth, "I was about to start an argument with my father when I felt someone saying I should love him," he continued, "but how can I love him after all he has done to us? How can I love him? I don't even like him."

No one spoke for some time. Then Kenneth asked, "Was that Jesus talking to me or was I just imagining it?"

"Oh, that was Jesus all right, Kenneth," said the Pastor with a smile. "You asked Jesus into your heart yesterday. You prayed to become more like Him. So Jesus is now a part of you. That is why you heard Him speaking to you. What He says is right. Jesus loves your father and you need to love him too."

"How can I do that?" asked Kenneth in surprise.

"You need the Holy Spirit to help you. You can't forgive your father right now, but Jesus will help you to learn how to forgive him. Just keep praying about it. I will be praying for you as well."

Over the next few months things did get better for Kenneth and his family. He didn't argue with his father. He found that sometimes he could help his father. Even his brother and sisters noticed a change in Kenneth. As the days passed Kenneth learned to be kind and helpful. It was not easy to learn to love his father but he kept praying about it. Every week Kenneth and his mother went to the Bible Teaching classes. He learned a lot about the stories in the Bible. Kenneth was a keen pupil and asked many questions.

One day the Pastor was reading the story of The Prodigal Son from the Bible in Luke 15:11-32. "I was just like the son in the story," Kenneth thought to himself as he pictured the son coming home to his father with no shoes on his feet and wearing dirty, torn clothes. Kenneth liked the part about the father watching for his son, then running to meet his lost son and kissing him.

"God welcomed me just as the father in the story had welcomed his son home," Kenneth said to the Pastor.

"Jesus wants to welcome back your father too, Kenneth," said the Pastor. Kenneth looked at him in amazement.

"You mean my father is like the Prodigal Son?" he asked.

"Yes, Jesus is waiting and longing for your father to return to Him. He will be forgiven. Your father will know God's love again."

When they got home he discussed this with his mother.

"Do you believe what the Pastor said today about Father? Would God really want him back?" Kenneth asked.

"Yes, I believe He does," his mother replied. "I've been praying for your father every night that he will turn back to God. When he is sorry for the wrong he has done, then God will forgive him. I know this is hard to understand and accept, but God accepted you, didn't He?"

Kenneth thought about this for some time but said nothing.

"Just ask God to help you pray for your father. God always hears our prayers and He will answer them," said his mother.

"I'll try, Mother," said Kenneth, "but it is hard."

Kenneth prayed for his father every night after that. He often thought about the Loving Father who wants to welcome back His lost followers. God was working in Kenneth's life.

Kenneth walks the ten miles to school with no shoes on

CHAPTER THREE

NEW HOPE

SOMETIME LATER Kenneth's father did return to God and the church. He stopped drinking and began to read his Bible again. Although he did get a job there was little money for clothes or shoes, but he did pay the school fees. Kenneth was allowed to sit the exams although he had lost a year of schooling. How surprised and happy he was when he passed! He started secondary school with his friends.

"Oh, I am so proud of you," said his mother on the day Kenneth started secondary school. "You have done really well to be accepted for higher education. Here, you will need these for the long journey to the city," she added as she handed him some bananas.

"Thanks, I don't know what time I'll be back home. I might have to go to the library to study the books I will need."

Kenneth put the bananas into his bag, put the bag on his shoulder and set off for school. Leaving early in the morning, he had to walk the ten miles to the school in his bare feet. He still had no shoes.

"What will the other students think of me?" he thought as he walked along the dusty road. "I can't hide the fact that

I have no shoes." He looked down at his dirty bare feet. "Ouch," he cried as his toe hit a stone on the road. Even though his feet were hard and used to walking on rough ground, he still often hurt his toes on a stone or jagged branch that was lying on the road.

"One day I will have a pair of shoes," he said to himself as he walked along the road. "I know God will provide me with shoes, just as the father in the story of the Prodigal Son gave his son the best shoes to wear."

Every day Kenneth walked along the hot dusty road to school, alone. He was the only day-pupil because his father couldn't afford the boarding fees. He walked to school in the rain. He walked to school in the heat. He walked to school every day with a smile on his face.

After some time Kenneth did get a pair of old thonged sandals to wear which helped a bit. Then, when he was nearly 15 years old, his father bought Kenneth a pair of shoes. How proud he felt as he left home for school that day. However, he was not very far along the road when he had to stop. His feet were hurting him. He was not used to wearing shoes!

"Just as well I didn't throw away the old sandals I've been wearing. I'll need them for walking along the road," Kenneth said to himself. "I'll keep my shoes for when I am in school. My feet will soon get used to them, but I won't spoil them by walking on the dusty road."

So Kenneth carried his new shoes to school every day and put them on when he got to the school. For four years he walked to school each day, while the other students lived at the school during the week.

He worked hard and after graduating from senior school he went to the Teacher's Training College in Kabale. After graduating with a Diploma in Education, Kenneth taught Religious Education and History at his local school. He thought that was the plan God had for his life. He would be a teacher and help other poor children to learn to read, then they could study the Bible for themselves. But God was not finished with Kenneth yet.

After a short time as a teacher, Kenneth got the chance to go to Scotland to study Theology. In 2000 he became a student at the International Christian College in Glasgow. God provided the fees for the course, plus the airfare through the giving of some generous people. Three years later Kenneth got his degree and returned to his hometown in Uganda. There he married Patricia and together they worked for their local church. Kenneth thought that was the plan God had for his life. God had provided him with a wife, a home, and a job. What more could he want? But God was not finished with Kenneth yet. He had greater plans for him.

One day the Pastor said to Kenneth, "I think God wants you to go to England and take another degree."

"How can I afford to go to England?" asked Kenneth, "I have no money to pay for my fees, and I will need to find somewhere to live. And what about my wife?" he added.

"God has provided for you in the past and if He wants you to go further then He will provide for you again," replied the Pastor.

Kenneth marvelled at the thought that God had more

work for him to do. He prayed about this idea, asking God to provide the money for a home and fees for this additional course.

God was faithful to Kenneth. He went to Cambridge to study, but it was many months before Patricia, his wife, could join him. He studied hard and passed all the exams. Before they returned to Uganda, God gave them the gift of a son, Daniel. From a little village in Rukengiri district to Glasgow, then Cambridge! Who could achieve all that except God alone? Through grace and much prayer Kenneth was enabled to do all that.

In November 2007 Kenneth became the Vicar at Emmanuel Cathedral, Kinyasano. He worked with the local people bringing them the Good News of Jesus. On Sunday 7th January 2009, Kenneth was ordained as Priest in the Anglican Church and his son Daniel was baptised on the same day.

Kenneth Karyaija, together with his wife Patricia, are currently mobilising their community in their home country of Uganda. They are trying to encourage the people to help themselves through sustainable development. They feel that education is the key to helping people out of poverty. In his hometown of Kiyaga, Kenneth preached the Gospel of Jesus Christ in both word and deed. They promoted good morals among the young people and tried to set an example to them. Patricia worked as Diocesan Accounts Officer in North Kegezi, as bookkeeper while studying part time.

His family home is once more a Christian home thanks to God who has worked faithfully with this family. Kenneth's father, Charles, is now a strong pillar of his local church and

Kenneth is ordained as a priest in the Anglican Church

is the missions' co-ordinator. Praise and singing have replaced alcohol. Many people in the community have come to the Lord because of Kenneth's and Charles' testimonies. Kenneth and Patricia now have a daughter, too.

In 2012, Kenneth was promoted to University Chaplain of Makerere University and Business School in Uganda's capital city, Kampala. He still preaches and now leads the congregation at St. James Chapel. Patricia is studying for a Postgraduate Diploma in Human Resource Management. What more has God got planned for Kenneth and his family? Only time will tell of God's mighty work in the future lives of Kenneth and Patricia. God alone has changed this family and brought them to serve Him for His glory.

Keep Taking the Tablets

CHAPTER ONE

HELPING HANDS

BRASIT LEFT HIS TRISHAW by the side of the road and fell down on the grassy bank. He tried to take a breath. His chest felt tight. He got onto his knees, bent forward, and then started coughing. When he finally stopped coughing Brasit slumped onto the grass. He felt so weak and could hardly breathe.

A friend, who was on his way to town, passed by.

"Are you all right, Brasit?" asked his friend Somsak when he saw Brasit lying on the grass by the side of the road. He went over to Brasit and helped him sit up. "You are not all right, are you?" he said looking at Brasit's face. "You need to see a doctor!"

Brasit shook his head and whispered, "No, no, I can't go

to the doctor. I have no money."

"But you are very ill," Somsak said desperately. "You need help."

Just then another friend, Eagle, came along the road pushing his bike up the hill.

"Has the hill been too much for Brasit?" he asked jokingly when he saw Brasit sitting on the grass.

"Brasit is very ill. He can hardly breathe," said Somsak. "He needs to go to the doctor but he says he can't because he has no money."

Eagle looked at Brasit. "Mm, he certainly looks bad. Can you stand up?" he asked Brasit.

Brasit shook his head, took out a dirty old handkerchief and coughed into it.

"He's coughing up blood!" said Somsak alarmingly, noticing the fresh blood on the handkerchief. "We need to get him to the hospital."

"Help me lift him up, Somsak," said Eagle, taking control of the situation. "Now let's carry him to his trishaw. We can take him to the hospital in the trishaw."

The two boys pushed the trishaw up the hill, after which Eagle hurried back for his bike. Somsak rode Brasit's trishaw while Eagle cycled behind him. When they got to the hospital they carried him into the emergency room. There they waited to hear what was to happen to their friend.

"I knew Brasit was not keeping well," said Eagle as they waited at the hospital. "He hadn't been at work all last week."

"Yes, he told me he had a cold but it is much more serious

than that, I'm afraid," replied Somsak. "He has not been able to work much this year. That is why he won't have any money for the doctor."

The two friends sat in silence for some time, then Somsak asked, "What will we do when they ask us for some money? I don't have any money, have you?"

"No, I don't have any money with me. We'll worry about that when the time comes. Let's just hope they can give him some medicine to make him better."

At last the doctor came. He sat down beside the two friends.

"I'm afraid I have bad news for you," he began, "your friend has TB. He is too ill for us to help him. The best thing you can do is take him home. We can do nothing for him and we don't want him to die here. Better to die at home." The doctor got up and looked at the two young boys. "Follow me," he said walking along the corridor.

Eagle and Somsak followed the doctor to a small dark room where Brasit was lying on the floor.

"You don't need to pay me for the examination," said the doctor as he left the room. "He is too ill—I don't expect he has any money to pay anyway."

They picked up their friend and carried Brasit out of the hospital. They put him in his trishaw and began the long journey back to where Brasit lived. On the way they stopped for a rest by some shady trees. They got some water for Brasit to drink. They sat there for some time.

"We can't just leave Brasit to die," said Somsak. "He has

no family to go to—surely there must be something we can do. He is too young to die."

"There may be one last chance," said Eagle. "I've been thinking about it all the way here."

"Well, what is it?" asked Somsak excitedly.

"There is this Christian Mission Hospital I heard about. One of the ladies working there was in my father's shop for some rice the other day. I heard her talking about the work they do there, helping poor people who are ill. Perhaps they could help."

Eagle got to his feet to give Brasit another sip of water. "What do you think about going to the Mission Hospital?" he asked Brasit as he held his head up to give him the water.

Brasit just nodded his head. He didn't care about anything now. The doctors at the hospital thought he was not worth the time or the effort or the cost to help him. He was too weak to help himself. All he could do now was to trust his friends.

"That's a great idea Eagle, isn't it Brasit?" said Somsak. "Come on, we will take him there right now while we have him in the trishaw."

With renewed energy the two friends began the journey to the Mission Hospital.

It was getting dark by the time they reached the Mission Hospital. The nurses were very kind and put Brasit into a bed in a ward. Eagle recognised the nurse who had come to his father's shop. She gave Eagle and Somsak some rice and told them they could stay with their friend sleeping under his bed, as was the custom.

The next morning, after a doctor had examined Brasit, the two boys had to go back to work. They said goodbye to their friend and left him in the care of the nurses.

"The doctor didn't hold out much hope for Brasit," said Somsak sadly as they made their way back to the city.

"Well, at least he will die in a nice place and the nurses will take care of him," said Eagle. "The missionary nurse who came to my father's shop said she would let us know how Brasit is getting on."

Brasit's two friends carry him into the Mission Hospital

CHAPTER TWO

A LITTLE BIT OF HOPE

SEVERAL WEEKS LATER the nurse from the Mission Hospital came into Eagle's father's shop. She told him that Brasit was still alive but that he had not yet responded to the injections they were giving him.

"As he has no friends or relatives to help him, it is difficult for him to get any food," she told Eagle's father. "The hospital has a policy of giving charity to poor patients if they get a letter from their village headman vouching for them. Perhaps Eagle could get a letter for Brasit?"

"Oh, thank you," replied Eagle's father, handing her the rice. "I will tell Eagle to go to the headman right away and get a letter for Brasit. Brasit was a monk for a while, you know. Our headman knows Brasit well. I'm sure he will recommend that Brasit needs help to pay for his medication and food."

"Good," said the nurse, "I can get the letter the next time I am in town. Remember we are all praying for him."

When Eagle was told about the letter, he ran to find Somsak to tell him the latest news of their friend.

"I am going to see the headman right away to get the letter from him," said Eagle.

"I hope the missionaries' prayers are better than ours. I have done all I can do," said Somsak sadly.

"At least he is still alive," replied Eagle.

"Yes, that's a good sign," replied Somsak. "The doctors here said he only had a few days to live. As long as he is alive there is hope."

"I hope the God they worship at the Mission Hospital hears the prayers for Brasit and answers them. I wonder if their God would help Brasit," said Eagle as he went off to find the village headman.

That night, at the Mission Hospital, Brasit too was wondering about this God that the missionaries were praying to about him. The doctor had told him he needed some milk. Where was Brasit going to get some milk up here in a hospital miles away from the city and his friends? Brasit had been thinking about this all day. Now in the quietness of the night Brasit prayed his first prayer to the missionaries' God: "God, I don't know you, but these missionaries here tell me that you love all people and want to be our friend. So if you are real, show me by bringing me some milk, please."

Brasit lay down and went to sleep, sure that no milk would arrive for him in the morning. He did hope, however, that his prayer might just have been heard and answered.

The next morning Brasit woke to the sound of someone shouting his name.

"Brasit, Brasit!" shouted one of the patients at the end of the ward. "There is some milk here for you! Someone left it here early this morning. Come and get it now."

Brasit could hardly believe what he just heard. He thought he must still be dreaming. He sat up in bed and shouted to the man at the end of the ward, "What did you say?"

"There's some milk here for you," came the reply, "come and get it."

Brasit wasted no time. He crawled out of bed and made his way slowly to the end of the ward where a tin of milk was sitting on the table by the door. A nurse came in and opened the tin pouring a little into a plastic mug. Brasit took a sip of the milk. It tasted lovely. He drank all the milk that was in the mug. The nurse poured some more milk into the mug and Brasit finished it in one gulp.

"Steady on, don't drink it all at once," said the nurse. "You would think you hadn't eaten for months the way you are drinking that milk!"

"Little do you know how true your words are," said Brasit as he put down the mug.

"I'll leave the tin of milk with you," said the nurse going up the ward to see to some of the patients. Brasit sat on the floor and slowly sipped the rest of the milk.

He thought that maybe it was just coincidence that the milk came. He didn't think it could happen a second time, but that night Brasit decided to try the prayer again. So he prayed, "Thank you God for the milk today, but I need more than just one day's milk, so could you please send me more tomorrow?"

The next morning there was another tin of milk for Brasit. The milk continued to arrive each morning and Brasit began to feel a lot stronger. The medicine, too, seemed to be helping now. Brasit was getting better.

A tin of milk for Brasit

One morning the milk didn't arrive. Brasit wondered what to do. He had told no one that he had prayed to the Christian God for the milk. Now he wondered if it had been God who had sent the milk for him. Later that day, as he was sitting on his bed watching the other patients talking with their families, a young lad came over to him.

"I'm staying here to help feed and look after my grandfather," said the young lad. "I have noticed that you don't have anyone to bring you food. Would you like to share some of our rice?"

Brasit could hardly believe his ears. Here was a complete stranger offering him some much needed food.

"Would you like some of our rice?" the young lad's words interrupted his thoughts.

"Yes please," said Brasit quickly. "That would be very kind of you. I have no one here to look after me as my friends live in the city. It is too far for them to come to visit me."

The young lad brought Brasit some of their rice.

Brasit could not sleep that night. He kept thinking about the young lad who offered to share his rice. He knew that, as he was getting stronger, he needed more than just milk. He needed food. He also realised that he was feeling really hungry. Brasit hadn't felt hungry for ages. Now God had provided food for him. He just had to believe that the Christian God was real and did care about people. The more he thought about it the more he knew he had to do something about it. So he decided to talk to the hospital evangelist the following day. He would tell him he wanted to know more about their God. He closed his eyes. For the first time in his life he felt at peace. As he fell asleep he prayed, "Thank you God for sending me the rice. I believe in you now and want to know more about you. Help me."

True to his word Brasit talked with the hospital evangelist about becoming a Christian. Every day the young lad shared their rice and vegetables with Brasit. When the missionary nurse came to visit him some days later, Brasit told her all about the milk and the food being shared by the young lad and his grandfather. He told her he had talked with the hospital evangelist and had decided to become a Christian.

Everyone was overjoyed at his decision.

"We are pleased you have decided to become a Christian and that you recognise that God has helped to make you well again," said the missionary nurse. "But remember, you still have a large bill to pay. Your friend was not able to get a letter from your village headman as he wanted to see you in person before he will say you are too poor to pay. As you can't leave the hospital yet, I don't know how we are going to solve this problem."

"I will pray about it," said Brasit confidently. "God will work it out, I am sure."

As the days went by Brasit became stronger and stronger. One day, after the doctor had examined Brasit, he told him, "We feel you are well enough now to leave the hospital. We have found you a place to live as you are still too weak to work. A Christian family we know will take care of you for a time. But remember, you can't leave the hospital till you have paid your bill for the medication and care you have had. We need the letter from your village headman before we can offer you any charity. It is just hospital policy."

Brasit wanted to leave the hospital and go to live with this family. He knew God had made him well but how was he going to pay this bill and also afford the injections he still needed to have every day?

One day a missionary friend of the family Brasit was to stay with, came to visit them. They told her about the problem with the hospital.

"I will go to the hospital administrator and explain Brasit's situation," she told them. "I am sure when I tell them that he was too ill to go to see his village headman for the letter they will understand. I will inform the hospital that he is really poor and has no means of paying this bill."

"Thank you," they said, humbly aware of how many people were helping Brasit.

A few days later the doctor came into the ward.

"I have great news for you, Brasit!" he said with a smile. "You can leave right away. You have been given 100% charity and enough injections for three months."

"Oh, praise the Lord!" shouted Brasit, jumping off his bed. "I knew God would work it out."

"You must go to the missionary nurses' home each morning for the injections," explained the doctor as Brasit got ready to leave.

Later that day Brasit was taken to the Christian family's house where he was to stay.

A typical home in a village in the country

CHAPTER THREE

LIFE IN THE CITY

THERE WAS A BIBLE in his new home so Brasit read it every day and prayed to God asking Him about his future. Every morning at 6 a.m. he went to the missionary nurse's house for his injection. Gradually his health improved. Soon he was able to take tablets instead of having injections.

"You have to keep taking the tablets for a year or you will not stay well," the missionary nurse told him. "Remember to come back for the next dose in a month's time. Everyone thought you were going to die when your friends brought you to our hospital. But God has a purpose for you, Brasit. God helped to make you better and the tablets will cure you completely."

Brasit was pleased to be free of having to go every morning for his injection. Soon Brasit felt strong enough to leave the Christian family and go back to his hometown. The family were sad to see him go. They gave him the Bible to keep, promising to pray for him every day. So Brasit went to live with Somsak and his family. He told everyone he met how God had helped him. Soon everyone heard about his miraculous cure. They were amazed that he had been saved from death by the doctors and nurses at the Mission Hospital. He continued to read his Bible when he had time, and he did pray occasionally.

"We thought we would never see you again," said Eagle one day when they met in the town. "Soon you will be able to push a trishaw up the hill again. I'm so glad the Christians' God helped you."

One day Brasit decided to go to Bangkok to try and find some work. Life in the big city was busy and enjoyable. Weeks passed. Brasit finished his pills. He felt fine so he didn't bother to go back for more.

"I'm better now," he said to himself. "I don't need to keep taking the tablets. I'll be fine."

Sometime later a friend met Brasit in the street.

"Brasit, a nurse from some Mission Hospital is looking for you. She came to my house asking if I knew where you were living."

"What did you tell her?" asked Brasit. "What did she want?"

"She said you had not come for your tablets and it was very important that you keep taking them," replied his friend.

"What tablets? I don't need any tablets now," said Brasit. "How did she know where to find me?"

"I don't know Brasit," said his friend. "All I know is that she is looking for you. She has come all the way here just to give you more tablets. Imagine anyone being that important! Special delivery for our Brasit," he said with a laugh.

"Really?" said Brasit feeling a bit foolish. "She came all the way here to give me more tablets?"

"Yes, and she was very insistent that you keep taking the tablets," said his friend.

"Oh dear, I never bothered to go back for more," said Brasit sadly. "I was too busy here in the city to take time to go home. Did she say where I would find her?"

"She said she was in Bangkok for a couple of days and would come back to my house with the tablets," replied his friend. "Come with me and hopefully she will have left the tablets for you."

As they hurried down the street his friend added, "They must be very special, these missionary nurses, coming all this way just to make sure you are all right."

That evening, as he lay in bed with the packet of tablets in his hand, Brasit realised that he was not completely cured. He knew how important it was to keep taking the tablets. He was amazed that a nurse from the hospital had come looking for him, just to give him the tablets! He thought about God and His love for people. Poor people, like Brasit, and even bad people, were loved by God. Brasit felt sad. He had let God down. He had let the mission nurses down. He had been too sure of himself, thinking he didn't need God now that he felt better. He couldn't sleep. He remembered the time he lay awake all night when he was in the hospital. He knew he had to do something. So he knelt down by the side of his bed and prayed: "Father God, forgive me for going my own way now that I am feeling better. I'm sorry that I forgot about you and the tablets, thinking I didn't need them, or you. Help me to be a better follower of your son Jesus. Show me the plan you have for my life."

The next morning he went straight to visit a relative whom he knew would know where the local Christian church was. He told him all about how ill he had been, about the Mission Hospital, and the missionary nurse coming to find him because he had stopped taking the tablets. His relative was so amazed at Brasit's story that he went with him to the church.

As they sat in the church tears streamed down Brasit's face as he realised just how much the Christian missionaries had loved him. Joy filled his heart as he felt the love of God flow over him. Brasit sensed God asking him to help bring others to know the love of God. After the service Brasit waited behind to speak to the Pastor. He told him his story and said that he wanted to serve God.

"What do I need to do to learn more about sharing God's love with others?" he asked the Pastor.

"You certainly have had an amazing experience of God's love for you. I'm sure the Holy Spirit is leading you to serving God," replied the Pastor. "I have some missionary friends here in Bangkok. I will arrange for you to meet with them. They will tell you what to do now."

Brasit met the missionaries and discussed his future with them. They suggested that he should go to Bible College to learn more about the Bible and the Christian faith. The next month Brasit packed his bags and went off to Bible College.

After a year at Bible College, Brasit met a young girl. They fell in love and were married. Brasit told her all about how God had saved him from certain death from TB.

"If it hadn't been for the care and medication given to me by the missionary nurses, I would not be alive today," he told her. "Now I want to serve God."

Through talking with a local missionary and being amazed at her husband's testimony she too came to trust in the Lord.

Together they have served the Lord in various churches in Central Thailand. Sometimes they worked with other missionaries, at other times they worked on their own among their own people. The Lord blessed them with three children. Being the Pastor to a small local Christian community meant that they had to rely on the giving of their congregation. It was often hard for them financially but they trusted God and He wonderfully provided for them. Although life was very hard for their children, all three grew up to trust and follow the Lord. They were good examples to their friends and proved their faith in school.

Brasit and his wife continue to pastor a church on the outskirts of the city where he lived and where he rode his trishaw. His eldest daughter became a missionary. She is now married with a daughter of their own. They too are serving the Lord, but that is another story of God's love and provision.

The small church and congregation

"I can't pretend to bow down," said Honey to herself.

Where is Your Security, Honey?

HONEY'S TESTIMONY

"JUST PRETEND you are worshiping the Buddha, Honey," whispered her friend Bird.

"I can't pretend," replied Honey quietly to her friend.

Honey and Bird were in the senior form at the local Secondary School. Every week the school assembled in the main hall for the Buddha Class. This was part of the school's religious programme and every pupil had to learn the chants and bow down to the monk three times. They had to listen to the monk and pray to the Buddha. The problem for Honey was that, as a Christian, she felt it wrong to worship the Buddha or the monk. So when all the students bowed down Honey kept sitting up. This was noticed by her teacher who told her she had to bow down or she would not pass the Buddhist exam.

The following week Honey knelt on the floor with the other pupils but when it came to the time to bow down Honey stayed on her knees, still sitting up.

"Oh no, the teacher is coming over to me," said Honey to herself as she sat there, the only head above the rest.

"Come with me to the headmaster's office right away," commanded the teacher angrily.

Honey stood up and followed the teacher. Her legs were shaking as she entered the headmaster's office.

"I thought it was explained to you that if you don't demonstrate that you know how to worship the Buddha you will not pass the exam," explained the headmaster, "and if you don't pass the exam you will not graduate."

"Sir, you know my father is a Christian Pastor," said Honey quietly. "I too am a Christian and I can't bow down and do the chants. I only pray to Jesus."

"Well, you know the consequences, Honey," replied the headmaster sternly. "It is up to you. If you think this Jesus is more important than getting your degree, then carry on the way you are doing. But I strongly advise you to follow our way."

Honey left the office in a dilemma. Getting her degree was very important to her. With a degree she could get a good job, earn lots of money, buy a fancy car and live in a big house. All these things Honey longed for. Being a Pastor's daughter was hard. There were few gifts and no money to buy nice things. They were reliant on the giving of their small congregation and there was never enough.

"Life was easy when I lived at home in our small village," Honey told her friend Bird as they walked back to the hostel. "As a child I just did what my parents told me to. We were known as Christians and went to our own church."

"But now you are free to do what you like, Honey," reminded Bird.

"I know, but that is what makes it more difficult," said Honey. "Away from my parents here in the city I can do what I want. No one will say anything, but I know in my heart that it is wrong."

"Why is it wrong?" asked Bird, trying to understand her friend.

"It's wrong because I am a Christian," replied Honey.

"When did you decide to become a Christian?" asked another friend. "Were you not just doing what your father wanted you to do?"

"No," replied Honey, "at first I thought I wanted to be rich as we were a very poor family. I decided I would become a Christian when I was older and had made a lot of money."

"Quite right," said Bird, laughing, "we all want to be rich someday."

"But then," continued Honey, "by God's grace I welcomed Jesus into my life when I was 12 years old. I felt God calling me to follow Him, and that He wanted me to be a missionary just like my father and aunties. I didn't want to be a missionary however, so I decided I would go to university and get a good degree first. Then I would think about what God wanted me to do."

"But what has all this to do with pretending to bow down to the Buddha so that you can pass your exams?" asked Bird.

"As a Christian I only worship God and He knows my heart," said Honey, trying to explain to her friends. "I have to trust God and please Him only. If I pass my exams but fail to honour God, I will gain nothing."

"Oh, I don't understand you, Honey," said Bird as she walked away.

Honey couldn't sleep that night. She worried about what her teacher would say to her. At first Honey thought she could disguise herself by bending backwards to hide behind her friends. Then the verse from the Bible, Matthew 10:32–33, came to mind:

> "Everyone who acknowledges me publicly here on earth, I will also acknowledge before my Father in heaven. But everyone who denies me here on earth, I will also deny before my Father in heaven."

As a young girl of 15 away from home Honey knew what she *should* do. Even if all the other girls agreed with Bird that she should just pretend to bow to the monk to pass the practical part of the exam, Honey felt this was wrong.

The next morning Honey found one of the ladies who looked after her in the girls' Christian Hostel. She knew this lady had been a Christian for a long time. Honey hoped she would advise her, so she told the lady about her dilemma.

"What do you think I should do?" Honey asked her.

"If I were you, Honey, I would do it just to pass the exam. After all, it is just part of your studies," the lady replied calmly.

Honey still felt it was not right. She couldn't get in touch with her father as they had no phone and they lived far away. What was she to do?

The following day Honey went to see her teacher.

"I'm sorry, but I can't bow down to the Buddha," said Honey.

"All right, Honey, you don't need to attend the class," replied the teacher.

However, some time later another incident occurred. When a teacher realised Honey was not attending the religious lesson she made her clean the room, and wash the utensils used for worship and have them ready for the next class.

For the next two months, every week, Honey washed and prepared the utensils for worship before the class, then cleaned the room afterwards, but she didn't attend the practical class. When the time came for the exams Honey sat the theory exam and passed! In fact, she got top marks in Buddhism, but she never bowed to the image of the Buddha.

After she finished high school Honey went on to University. She didn't have any problem with Buddhism there because she didn't need to take that module. During the fourth year at University Honey felt God calling her again to be a missionary. She didn't want to follow this call because she had already decided to get a good job so that she could make a lot of money. Still, God challenged Honey with the question, "Where is your security?"

After four years at University Honey, now 21, got her degree in Food Science and looked forward to a job which would bring her riches. Before starting to look for a job Honey got the chance to visit friends in Germany. While she was with them, they encouraged her to follow God's calling on her life. So, when she went back home, she prayed about this. In the meantime she got a job as a management trainee in an ice cream parlour. She worked there for ten months but she still felt restless. She was certain God was calling her to be a missionary, but she was not sure she wanted to be a missionary. One night as she prayed she felt God asking her again, "Where is your security, Honey?"

In the past Honey looked to herself for security. She thought that a first class education, followed by a good, reliable job would bring her lots of money. Money and hard work would give her all the security she needed, she thought. But God was calling her and He told her, "I am your real security. You will never find security in material possessions. If you love me, trust and obey me. I will never leave you or fail you. I know the plans I have for you."

Honey got out her Bible and looked up Jeremiah 29:11-13. There it was, the very words God had spoken to her! –

"For I know the plans I have for you," declares the LORD, "plans to prosper you and not to harm you, plans to give you hope and a future. Then you will call on me and come and pray to me, and I will listen to you. You will seek me and find me when you seek me with all your heart." (*Jeremiah 29:11-13 NIV.*)

She knew then that she too wanted to be a missionary just as God had planned. Now she looked to Jesus. She knew that

God had given her His promise. So she gave up her original plan and surrendered all to Him.

"I know God is calling me to be a missionary," Honey told her parents some time later. "I think I need to go to the UK and learn English."

"How are you going to get to the UK?" asked her sister when the family came together to discuss this.

"I don't know," replied Honey, "but if God wants me to go to England, He will make it possible."

God did make it happen. Some weeks later He opened the door for Honey to go to England to work and study English.

Before the family knew it, Honey was on her way to Exeter where she worked as a volunteer at a Christian Centre in Devon. For ten months she learned to read and write English while clearing tables, washing dishes and cleaning the Centre. It was while Honey was there that it was suggested she apply to the International Christian College in Scotland to study Theology with a view to becoming a missionary.

Honey came to the UK with nothing apart from God. Amazingly, God provided everything she needed! So God *was* her support and the Bible *was* her bank statement.

One day, before Honey left Devon to go to Glasgow, some friends asked her if she had the money for the fees.

"God will provide!" Honey told them even though she was shaking and had many doubts. She was very anxious and still had a lot of unanswered questions. That night, as she did every night, Honey walked slowly home up the hill. Quite unexpectedly, her neighbour, a 90-year-old man called Frank, called to her from his garden.

"Honey, we want to speak to you," said Frank, "come on in."

As Honey came into the garden Frank said, "I hear you are going to Scotland to study the Bible."

Frank led Honey over to the bench beside his house. His wife was sitting there waiting for them.

"Have you got the money for the fees, dear?" asked Frank's wife.

"Not yet," replied Honey, "but I know God is a loving Father who supplies all our needs. If He wants me to go to ICC then He will provide the money."

Frank looked at Honey and said, "This morning while my wife was having her quiet time with God, He told her to help you before you went to Scotland."

As Frank handed Honey the envelope containing £200 he said, "Honey, please remember, sometimes it seems God works slowly or that He is not working at all, but His help will never be late. It is always on time. It's just because He wants to teach His children to trust Him fully."

At that time Honey felt that the *amount* of money was not important for her; what was important was that God had confirmed that she was doing His will. God was with her and He would never forsake her.

So at the age of 24, with very limited English, Honey went to ICC to study for three years for a degree in Theology. The first term exams were very difficult but with hard work and a lot of help from staff and fellow students, she passed them all. By the end of the second term she had settled into life at the college and had made many friends.

Life was very busy at ICC as students and staff prepared for the next set of exams. One day Tricia, a fellow student, found Honey crying outside a classroom.

"What's the matter, Honey?" she asked. "Why are you crying?"

Through her sobs Honey replied, "I have to go back home. My Visa has been turned down. I have to leave right away."

"Right away!" said Tricia in astonishment. "What about your exams?"

By this time several other students had gathered round wondering why the usually happy and smiling Honey was crying.

"Honey has to leave the country right away," announced Tricia to the gathering crowd.

At the worship service later that day staff and students prayed that Honey would be granted her Visa and would be able to return to Scotland after the Easter break. With great sadness everyone wished Honey well, promising to pray for her as she left.

"Do you think Honey will be granted a Visa?" asked one of the students.

"We can only pray about it," replied Tricia. "It is all in God's hands. But you would have thought they would have let her sit her exams first before ordering her out of the country like an illegal immigrant!"

"Well, at least she will get to be with her family for Easter," said Anne, another friend. "It will be nice for her to be home for a while."

"But will she get back?" asked Tricia. "That's the point."

After the Easter break all the students and staff met in the worship area for the beginning of term service. To everyone's surprise Honey walked into the room. Not only had Honey been granted her Visa for a further three years' study, she had also been given the fare to return to Glasgow!

After the first year at college with her exams behind her, Honey recognised that God had provided everything she needed, both materially and spiritually. During the summer holidays Honey got a job working in a guest house which gave her some money towards what God had already provided for her.

"I can truly say with the psalmist that 'My help comes from the Lord, the Maker of heaven and earth,'[3]" she told her friends.

During her final year at ICC Honey met and fell in love with Gerard, a fellow student from Switzerland.

Honey's parents, sister and brother came over to be with Honey when she graduated with a BA in Theology with Cross-Cultural Ministry. They met Gerard and spent some time together although it was difficult communicating.

To help teach English to foreign students, Honey went to

3. Psalm 121:1, 2.

a further education college for a year so she would gain her proficiency level grade in English. Life was hard at this college as Honey met students from different backgrounds. Once again she seemed to be the only Christian in her class. She found the attitude and behaviour of some of the young students difficult to understand. This was a tough year for her but, again, she passed all her exams.

Honey and Gerard dated for six months before Honey had to return home where she worked for a year with her father in his small church. Gerard wanted to marry Honey but Honey felt that God had given her a heart for the people of Mongolia. Gerard didn't think he had the same call as Honey, so he ended the relationship. Once again with many tears Honey and Gerard parted. Honey went to Mongolia as a missionary and Gerard returned home to work in Switzerland.

Life as a single girl in a cold, poor country was difficult for Honey. The culture was so different from her own warm, friendly culture or from the culture she had grown to know and like in the UK. She worked with the young people in Mongolia while she tried to learn their language. She was strict with the young people but was also very fair.

After two years studying the language it was time for Honey to decide her future. She prayed that God would guide her about what she should do. Would she return to Mongolia to work with the young people? Or would she teach English, or co-edit a Mongolian grammar book which

Life was difficult in this cold, poor and different country

would help other missionaries with their studies? What did God want her to do?

Honey set aside a day for praying and fasting as she sought what God had planned for the next part of her life. As she began her quiet time with the Lord, she felt God asking her to pray for Gerard. "Where had this thought come from?" she wondered. It certainly couldn't have come from God nor could it have come from her own thoughts. Honey hadn't thought about Gerard for two years.

"How can I pray for someone who is out of my life now?" she asked God. "I have had no letters, emails or phone calls—nothing."

Her heart ached as thoughts of Gerard come flooding

back. She thought she had got over him. She thought she would never find another one to love. She wondered how he was getting on.

"I can't pray for Gerard," said Honey quietly as she knelt in prayer that November morning. But every time she tried to pray for something else she felt God telling her to pray for Gerard.

"Okay, God, if you want me to pray for Gerard, I will. Get it over with, then I can concentrate on what *You* want me to do," Honey prayed. Then she thought, "What should I pray about for him?"

The more she thought about it the more she didn't know what to pray for. Honey searched her Bible for help—nothing. Eventually Honey got down on her knees and prayed:

"Please, help Gerard to grow with you, Lord, and let him know your will in his life. I pray that you will give him the courage to follow your will." Honey knew that there was no point in Gerard knowing God's will if he was not going to follow what God asked. Then Honey continued to pray, "Please, Father God, give him a Godly wife who can help and support him so that they may grow in faith together."

Honey continued to pray for the rest of the day and felt a peace she hadn't felt for some time. She knew God was guiding her and helping her.

That night an amazing and unexpected thing happened. An email came from Gerard explaining about how God had been working gently in his life and how God was drawing *his heart* to Mongolia! He then asked Honey to think carefully about what he said in the email. If she wanted to she could call him to discuss this. So, while Honey had been praying for Gerard in Mongolia, God had been speaking to Gerard in Switzerland! Gerard now felt God calling him to Mongolia, so he sent the email to Honey. He still loved her, he said, and wanted to marry her. He wondered if she still loved him—or had she found someone else?

Honey could not believe it! She wasn't happy or excited about receiving this email from Gerard, but was in shock and confused about what she should do. Her heart was full of fear as she didn't want to be hurt again.

She decided to go to her missionary friends and seek their prayers and advice. All her friends and fellow missionaries prayed to God asking Him to show both Honey and Gerard what His plans were for their lives. Honey asked God to show her if this was His plan. She needed confirmation about whether this was the step He wanted her to take.

The following day she phoned Gerard. As she was due to go to Scotland for Christmas they decided to meet back in the UK to discuss this change of heart.

While in Scotland God graciously showed Honey that this was His will for her. This gave her the confidence to accept Gerard's proposal of marriage.

After much prayer Honey returned home to prepare for her marriage to Gerard. Gerard joined her some months later. Honey's family gave them a beautiful, meaningful, traditional Christian wedding. After spending a few weeks with Honey's family they returned to Switzerland for another ceremony for Gerard's family. Many friends from the UK and those who couldn't travel to Asia joined them for the celebrations. A happy Christian home was set up in Switzerland as Gerard continued to work while Honey studied French. Following much prayer and discussion Gerard went through the process with the missionary society.

Honey and Gerard are now in Mongolia with their little daughter. Together they are learning the language while working with the local church. Never in her wildest dreams did Honey think that God would work things out for good in such an amazing way, but as the Apostle Paul says in Romans 8:28:

> "And we know that in all things God works for the good of those who love him, who have been called according to his purpose." (*Romans 8:28 NIV.*)

Once again God has shown Honey how He wants her to share in His work of spreading the Good News of Jesus. There will be ups and downs as Honey and Gerard seek to do God's work. Things will not always work out as they want. Life will be hard for them wherever God sends them, but they have learnt to trust God and rely on His strength to get them through. There will be times of urgent prayer, times of hard decision-making and times of wondering what to do next. There will also be many blessings and times of joy as they follow God's plan for their lives. God hasn't finished with them yet. He still has much work for them to do, but they both know He is with them all the time, directing all they do for His Glory.

Honey learned to love these people

Discussion

The following sets of ideas and questions provide an opportunity to think about each story more and bring out ideas of similar topics from the Bible. You can also enjoy these stories with a group of adults or with children in a Sunday School setting, to talk about becoming a Christian. The wondering questions can be used to help you and/or other members of the discussion group to identify with each story.

1. Chitra's story: 'Watch Out for the Monkeys!'

At the end of this story take the opportunity to think further about it or discuss it in a group, bringing in a story from the Bible. For example the story about Peter saying he didn't know Jesus. Here Peter is seen weeping because he had let Jesus down but Jesus used him greatly later on. This story can be found in Matt. 26: 69-75; Mark 14:66 -72, and Luke 22:54-62. John 21: 15-17 could also be read. Use these wondering questions to help identify with the story.

1. I wonder how Chitra and his sister felt when they realised they had to stay in the old hut in the middle of the forest.

2. Have you ever been scared somewhere?

3. What part of the story did you like best?

4. How do you feel when you have done something wrong?

5. Was there a difference between the way the village people reacted to Sundar's death and the way his Christian friends reacted?

6. When do you think Chitra knew God was calling him to become a Christian?

7. Where do you think Chitra got the money to go to the UK to learn English and to study?

8. What do you think it was like for Chitra living away from home and family in Scotland?

9. How do you think he managed to study there?

10. Who helped Chitra make his desire to build a church, an orphanage and a school come true? (How many people can you think of?)

11. Why did Chitra make the CD?

12. I wonder what else God wants Chitra to do for His glory in the future?

2. Kenneth's story: 'No Shoes'

At the end of this story an opportunity is given to discuss it more and bring in similar topics from the Bible. For example the story about the Prodigal Son or the Loving Father, found in Luke 15, could be read. You can also use this story to talk about becoming a Christian. Then use the wondering questions to help identify with the story.

1. I wonder how the family felt hiding in the banana plantation all night.

2. What did Kenneth think when he couldn't go to school because his father hadn't paid the school fees?

3. What part of the story did you like best?

4. Who helped Kenneth forgive his father?

5. What influence were his mother, the Pastor and the Holy Spirit?

6. Do you need to forgive someone who has hurt you?

7. How do you think Kenneth felt when he got a pair of shoes?

8. When did you get something you longed for and what was it?

9. Have you ever felt you were different from other people because of your faith?

10. How did the prayers of his family and the Pastor help Kenneth's father change from spending all the money on drink to praising the Lord?

11. Why did Kenneth have the confidence to go to
    Scotland to study when he had no money?

12. Has God got a plan for you too?

3. Brasit's story: 'Keep Taking the Tablets'

At the end of this story take the opportunity to discuss it
more and bring in similar topics from the Bible. For example
the story about the four friends bringing the man on a
stretcher to Jesus, found in Mark 2:1-12, Matt. 9:2-8, or
Luke 5:17-26, could be read. You can also use this story to
talk about becoming a Christian. The wondering questions
will help identify with the story.

1. I wonder how Brasit felt when the doctor told
   him to go home to die.

2. Who helped Brasit and why did they help him?

3. Why was the Mission Hospital different?

4. What part of the story did you like best?

5. Have you ever been very ill?

6. How did you get better?

7. When do we need to help our friends or family?

8. I wonder how Brasit felt when the milk
   arrived for him.

9. What do you think God is like?

10. How do you feel about God?

11. What made Brasit decide to follow Jesus?

12. Where do you go to for help when you are
    sad or in trouble?

4. Honey's story: 'Where is Your Security, Honey?'

At the end of this story an opportunity is given to discuss it
more and bring in similar topics from the Bible. For example
the stories about Paul's missionary journeys from Acts Ch.9
onwards tell of the trials and difficulties of being a
missionary. You can also use this story in a group setting to
talk about becoming a Christian. Talk through the
wondering questions to help identify with the story.

1. I wonder what Honey felt when the teacher saw that
   she was not bowing down to the Buddha.

2. Why was it difficult for Honey to pretend to bow down
   to the Buddha?

3. Have you ever had to pretend or tell lies?

4. When have you been afraid to be different from your
   friends?

5. What part of the story did you like best?

6. Who helped Honey make the decision to go to
   Mongolia rather than getting married?

7. Where or to whom do you go when you need help?

8. I wonder what it was like for Honey living alone in Mongolia.

9. Why was Honey not happy when Gerard told her God was calling him to go to Mongolia?

10. How do you think Honey and Gerard felt about going to Mongolia with their baby daughter?

11. Do you think things will be easier in Mongolia now that Honey has her own family with her?

12. What country would you like to visit?